READY TECHNOLOGY

Fast-Tracking New Business Technologies

READY TECHNOLOGY

Fast-Tracking New Business Technologies

Stephen J. Andriole

CRC Press
Taylor & Francis Group
Boca Raton London New York

CRC Press is an imprint of the
Taylor & Francis Group, an **informa** business

AN AUERBACH BOOK

CRC Press
Taylor & Francis Group
6000 Broken Sound Parkway NW, Suite 300
Boca Raton, FL 33487-2742

First issued in hardback 2017

© 2014 by Taylor & Francis Group, LLC
CRC Press is an imprint of Taylor & Francis Group, an Informa business

No claim to original U.S. Government works

Version Date: 20141217

ISBN-13: 978-1-4822-5576-8 (pbk)
ISBN-13: 978-1-138-44027-2 (hbk)

Library of Congress Cataloging-in-Publication Data

Andriole, Stephen J.
    Ready technology : fast-tracking new business technologies / Stephen J. Andriole.
        pages cm
    Includes bibliographical references and index.
    ISBN 978-1-4822-5576-8 (pbk. : alk. paper) 1. Information technology--Management.
    2. Business enterprises--Technological innovations. 3. Technological
    innovations--Economic aspects. I. Title.

    HD30.2.A5358 2015
    658.5'14--dc23   2014027302

Visit the Taylor & Francis Web site at
http://www.taylorandfrancis.com

and the CRC Press Web site at
http://www.crcpress.com

Contents

Executive Summary

Ready technology is a new category of information technology (IT). Ready technology sits between—and contributes to both—operational and strategic technology (Figure ES.1).

Ready technology replaces a lot of the "emerging technology" that was—and often still is—adopted at a slow and steady pace. Emerging technology is often perceived as "research and development (R&D)," "innovation," and potentially even "disruptive." Emerging technology is tracked and studied, and after a deliberate period of due diligence, is carefully piloted and sometimes even deployed. The process is generally very slow (years versus months, or even weeks).

Ready technology is emerging technology on steroids. *The major distinctions between emerging technology and ready technology include (a) the length of the due diligence process, (b) the importance of early requirements validation, and (c) fundamental assumptions around the technology adoption process itself, among some other differences that present opportunities to improve business processes very quickly and very cheaply.*

In fact, ready technology is *ready* because it is

- Out-of-the-Gate "Mature"
- Requirements Agnostic
- Usually Delivered from the Cloud

Figure ES.1   The range of technologies.

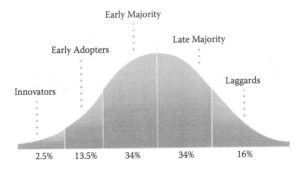

Figure ES.2   The technology adoption curve. (Rogers, Everett M., *Diffusion of Innovations.* New York: Free Press, 1962).

- Fast and Cheap
- Risk Neutral

Ready technology challenges 20th century technology adoption models that were (and still are) so popular among technology buyers, especially traditional technology buyers in large organizations. Originally developed by Everett Rogers (1962), the technology adoption curve describes the process by which companies *still* vet technology investment decisions. "Innovators" are the earliest adopters; "laggards" are the slowest. As Figure ES.2 suggests, the percentages are interesting, especially since only 16% are ready technology adopters (the innovators *and* early adopters), *68% are part of the early/late majority adopters,* and 16% are laggards. If we look at the adoption in companies of iPads, social media, and "bring your own device" (BYOD) policies alone, we see much earlier technology adoption rates. In fact, it was reported that *93% of Fortune 100 companies adopted iPads immediately after they were introduced.**

---

* Apple reported that 93% of Fortune 500 companies have deployed or are testing iPads. (Sean Ludwig, "The iPad Is an Incredible Tool for Work—If Your IT Department Will Allow It," *VentureBeat,* January 4, 2012 [http://venturebeat.com/2012/01/04/ipad-enterprise-it/#sZBVhhB7uxj1vk4U.99, accessed August 7, 2013].)

Such a rate of adoption is unprecedented—*or is it?* Are more and more technologies finding their way into more and more households and companies faster and faster? What is the trajectory of technology adoption?

The technology adoption curve is predicated on technology capability (and, as with just about everything, a little bias). The conventional assumption is that technology *evolves* at a pace that justifies *phased* adoption. Early deployments are assumed to be risky—but *potentially* have a high payoff—because the technology is likely not fully baked. Later adoption is safer, especially if a company is part of the "early" or "late" majority (the 68%) and has prior experience that justifies their approach to technology adoption—that is, they have not "suffered" because they were "late" (or they were once "punished" because they were early).

The adoption curve also assumes up-front due diligence requirements where business requirements are well understood and well defined before candidate technologies are vetted. This is the essence of the old technology adoption curve: *requirements first/technology second.* Many of us tried to perfect the requirements-first/technology-second adoption model (Andriole, 1987, 1992, 1996). The business technology field itself devoted countless articles, books, and conferences to the "requirements problem," "business technology alignment," and "requirements modeling" platforms. It all made sense back then, and aspects of the requirements-first/technology-second adoption model still make some sense today. But things are also different now: there are immediate business opportunities that ready technologies present to even the most conservative technology adopters. Some of these "opportunities" are relatively well understood, while others are to be discovered (TBD). *What this means in practice is that a specific technology, or even a basket of technologies, may well be adopted without any specific problems in mind.* The assumption is that technologies like tablets, social media, and analytics will quickly solve some problems, even if the problems are unclear *or even unknown* at the time of adoption.

Ready technology adoption is related to, but different from, the adoption "chasm" described by Geoffrey A. Moore (1991). Moore argues that there is a chasm between early adopters and the early majority that must be managed by high-tech marketers. "Ready" is quite different from the "chasm" because ready technology is low cost and low risk. Ready is not a conundrum that requires specialized marketing.

In addition to the high maturity level of many ready technologies, a major distinction between emerging and ready technologies is requirements discovery. Traditional technology adoption models were driven by detailed—and "validated"—requirements definitions. But today's adoption models are often driven by *initial requirements ignorance*, heresy to many technology buyers.

The approach assumes that technologies should drive requirements—not the other way around—which is why ready technologies are "discovered" through deployment instead of defined before technologies are deployed. Marchand and Peppard (2013) make the same case regarding analytics projects. They describe what they call "discovery-driven project management" as including the following steps:

- Develop Theories
- Build Hypotheses
- Identify Relevant Data
- Conduct Experiments
- Refine Hypotheses in Response to Findings
- Repeat the Process

They argue that successful technology deployments are discovered not managed, and that companies should "experiment" with technologies until they find the right combination of requirements and technologies, *which is the essence of the ready argument made here.*

Operational technology can be "ready"; strategic technology can be "ready." Ready technology is deployable quickly and cheaply. Ready technology is technology that has achieved a level of maturity that makes it operationally or strategically ready for business, even if the details of the requirements are poorly understood.

Operational and strategic requirements can be known *or* discovered—ready technology can go both ways. Operational technology includes the infrastructure basics (Figure ES.3). Strategic technology is more outward facing and much less about technology plumbing (Figure ES.4).

Ready technology can be transformative or just part of the "normal" innovation process. The keys are performance (against a set of known or to-be-discovered requirements), speed, and cost.

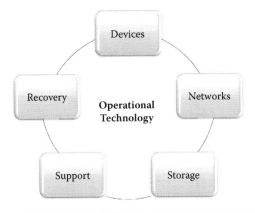

Figure ES.3 Operational technology.

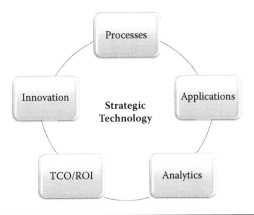

Figure ES.4 Strategic technology.

The ready technology adoption process is fast, cheap, and potentially extremely impactful. Examples include the immediate adoption of iPads, BYOD delivery models, cloud-based delivery, and the rapid adoption of social media listening/engagement technologies. It is now possible to immediately and cheaply pilot and deploy these and other ready technologies. The availability of ready technology is changing the way we think about technology adoption, business problem solving, and agility. The key is to move fast, spend as little money as possible, and free yourself of the requirements "burden" that constrains the rapid deployment of ready technologies: if you pilot, they will come.

Traditional technology adoption processes need to adapt to ready technology and the premise that ready technologies can dramatically, and immediately, impact business models and processes. Ready technology requires processes designed to continuously and quickly see/deploy/assess ready technologies. It also requires organizations to work horizontally, because ready technologies can impact corporate functions, processes, strategies, and, ultimately, effectiveness.

Ready technology *today*—and it will certainly change over time—looks like the depiction in Figure ES.5.

The essence of ready organization, processes, and governance is the formalization of ready technology assessment and exploitation. The "rules" around all this are important especially since they (re-)define a company's technology culture.

For many companies this all represents a huge change in the way they see technology, in the way they track/acquire/pilot/deploy/assess/support technology, and how they define agility (if they define agility at all). Learning how to almost instantly and seamlessly identify, pilot, and deploy ready technologies is a skill that must be developed.

Figure ES.6 presents enterprise and business unit perspectives on how and where ready technology assessments should occur. The figure suggests that ready technology assessments and formal due diligence should serve both the enterprise and business units. Note also that the technologies should be assessed with an equally pernicious assessment

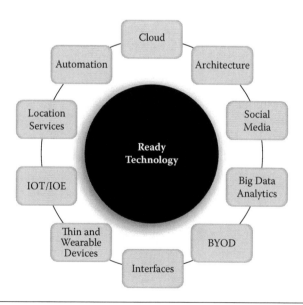

Figure ES.5   Ready technology.

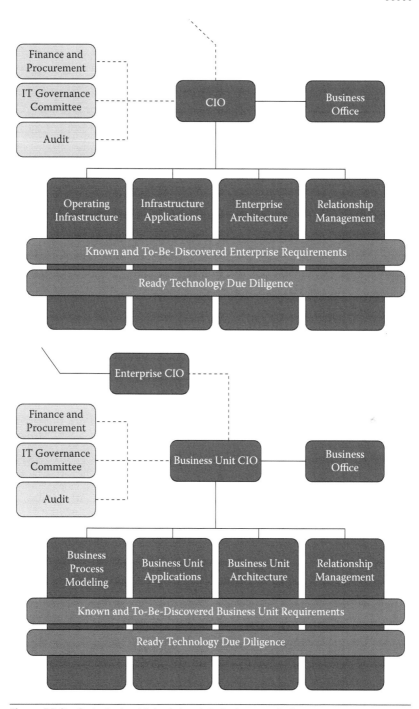

Figure ES.6 Centralized and federated ready technology organizations.

of business requirements. *In fact, these "requirements TBD" should be reassessed with reference to ready technologies and not just the mature technologies we tend to correlate with well-understood business requirements.*

The teams that comprise these new organizations should pursue the following tasks:

- Organize for Ready Technology
- Track Technology Trends
- Vet Promising Ready Technologies
- Pilot the Most Promising Technologies
- Deploy Ready Technologies Across the Enterprise and/or Business Units
- Measure the Impact of Ready Technologies
- Continuously Repeat the Process

The tasks first require ready teams to organize to optimize the ready technology opportunity. They then require companies to formally track technology trends. This requires the ongoing tracking of the research and development (R&D) budgets of technology vendors, where the venture capital industry is placing its bets, and how *Wall Street* defines forward value. It also requires relationships with all of the technology research organizations, pundits, and bloggers. It assumes a lot of conversations and even more travel. It assumes personnel, budgets for research, consultants, and travel and prestige. (The last assumption—*prestige*—is important: the smartest people at the company should want to be members of the ready team. If the best and brightest avoid the ready mission, it will fail.)

Ready teams must vet ready technologies.

A set of criteria should be used to determine a technology's potential. Here are 10 criteria for vetting ready technologies:

- Is the Technology on the Right Technology/Market Trends Trajectory?
- Is the Technology an R&D Target for the Largest Technology Vendors?
- Is the Technology a Target for the Private Equity Venture Community?
- Is the Technology Driving Wall Street Valuation Models?

- Does the Technology Have a Minimal Infrastructure Requirements Story?
- Is the Technology Cost-Effective (TCO)?
- Is the Technology Quantitatively Impactful (Return on Investment [ROI])?
- Does the Technology Have a Clear Differentiation Story?
- Can the Technology Be Delivered Via the Cloud?
- Are Competitors Vetting the Technology?

These criteria are representative of the kinds of evaluative clusters that companies can use to vet all varieties of ready technologies.

The methodology should be as structured as possible, as suggested in Figure ES.7.

The technologies that score the highest should be immediately piloted, and those that pilot well should be immediately deployed. The *governance* around all this is critical. Technology governance, like all corporate governance, is about decision/input rights that describe who is allowed to acquire, deploy, and support business technology. In fully centralized technology organizations, all of the decision rights belong to the centralized control group; in decentralized organizations, decision rights are diffuse; and in federated technology organizations, rights are shared. Companies must decide what works for their industry, leadership, and corporate culture. But without clear, consistent technology governance, companies will—at great

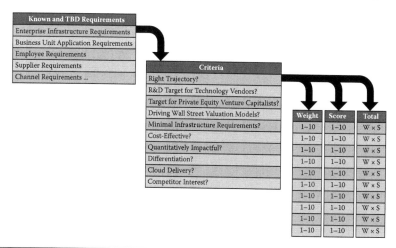

Figure ES.7 Ready technology assessment methodology.

risk—underinvest or overinvest in digital technology and inevitably miss important ready opportunities.

The empowerment aspect of governance is what unleashes technology's contribution to growth and profitability. If managers and executives can make the right ready technology investments at the right time, without the constraint of rigid governance structures and processes, technology's contribution to the business can be significant. Figure ES.8 suggests what governance should look like in a federated organization. Note that ready technology is co-owned by the enterprise and business units. This is consistent with the horizontal power of ready technologies (see Figure ES.6).

The governance of ready—and all—technology is critical to the successful piloting and deployment of technology. We are well beyond centralized technology acquisition/deployment/support, well beyond 20th century technology governance. *Federated governance, especially in the era of ready technology, is the only way to exploit operational and strategic ready technology opportunities.* The key to the exploitation of ready technology is organizational and requirements flexibility. The old sequential technology acquisition/deployment/support processes will never survive the pace of technology change and the volatility of global competition. Companies need to be able to move as quickly as possible to pilot/deploy ready/evolving technologies that will keep them competitive.

Ready technology is real *and* perceived. Many of today's new technologies are more than ready for deployment. But many managers and executives believe that new technology is inherently risky. The ready argument assumes some major differences between the old "new" technology and emerging *ready* technology. These differences should be explored and discovered through pilots designed to measure the contribution these technologies can make to business problem solving.

Areas Actors	Enterprise Architecture	Operating Infrastructure	Business Applications	Ready Technology
Enterprise CIO	Decision Rights	Decision Rights	Input Rights	Decision and Input Rights
Business Unit CIOs	Input Rights	Input Rights	Decision Rights	Decision and Input Rights

Figure ES.8   Technology governance.

Defined Adoption	*Ready* Adoption	Implications	Examples
• Defined Business-Driven Requirements Analysis and Validation • Full Technology Pilot Demonstrations Prior to Deployment • Required Integration of New Technology into Existing Technology Architectures • Transition Period to Test and Integrate New Technology • Continuous Support and Refresh Requirements	• Defined and Undefined Consumer-Driven Requirements Analysis and Exploration • Uncontrolled, Ad Hoc Technology Pilots • Limited or No Integration of New Technology into Existing Technology Architectures • Immediate Adoption and Delivery through Cloud Providers • Limited Support and Refresh Requirements	• Accelerated Technology Adoption • Increase in "Fail Fast/Fail Cheap" Pilots • Rapid Technology-Driven Business Process Change • Improved Technology TCO/ROI, Especially through the Avoidance of Large Integration, Support, and Refresh Costs • Major Changes in Corporate Governance of Information Technology	• BYO: Devices, Applications, Data, etc. • Tablets (such as iPads) • Smartphones (such as iPhones and Androids) • Content/File Sharing (with, e.g., Dropbox) • Mobile Applications (from App Stores) • Social Networking (with Facebook, Twitter, Flickr, etc.) • Video-Teleconferencing (with Facetime, Skype) • Video Sharing and Marketing (with YouTube) • Location Awareness (with, e.g., Foursquare)

Figure ES.9   *Defined* versus *Ready* technology adoption.

The list of ready technologies will continue to grow. The 10 clusters discussed here should be piloted and deployed, but they will also be followed by an ever-changing set of technologies ready, willing, and able to go to work. A commitment to watching and researching emerging technologies and adding them to the ready list should become a core competency. The power of ready technologies and their potential to change the way your company does business is wide and deep. Given how relatively inexpensive the technologies are to pilot and deploy, there is enormous leverage in the development and implementation of a ready strategy. You can count on your vendors, employees, customers, suppliers, and partners to help you exploit ready technologies.

Today, many emerging technologies are ready for immediate deployment. iPads are ready. Dropbox is ready. Skype is ready. ListenLogic is ready. Foursquare is ready. Ready technology is accessible and cost-effective. *It also often arrives at companies without the participation of the corporate IT team, especially in federated or decentralized companies where business units and employees are encouraged to solve their own problems.*

Figure ES.9 summarizes *defined* and *ready* technology adoption and the implications of ready technology adoption.

Introduction

Disconnect everyone from e-mail, the Web, software applications, and the databases they use all day (and night) to do their jobs (and live their lives). See how long it takes for the help desk to light up with angry employees threatening to do all sorts of unspeakable things to you and your technology providers. Then disconnect your customers and suppliers and see how long it takes for revenue to crash. Just for fun, stop upgrading your laptops, tablets, and smartphones, or worse, destandardize all the machines in the enterprise. Avoid migration to the cloud, disdain mobility's role, and declare social media, big data analytics, and location-based services fads that will be gone in a couple of years.

Of course no one would disconnect employees, suppliers, and customers from their digital worlds just to prove a point about how dependent everyone is on their digital tools and toys: we already know how completely dependent we all are on the technology that now defines who we are, what we do, and how companies make money. The arguments in the early 21st century about the fading importance of information technology (IT) were silly then and are ridiculous today. Yes, a lot of technology has been commoditized and operational technology is now available from a variety of low-cost providers. But business operations and strategies are simply lost without IT. *In fact, all of the major strategic and tactical challenges that companies face today are ultimately solved by some form of digital technology.*

While operational technology has indeed commoditized, our dependence on operational and strategic technology is so complete that it is impossible to separate business from technology—or technology from business.

Since 2000, there have been a series of challenges about the value of IT, about whether or not IT is still really important. Paul Strassmann (http://www.strassmann.com) has argued for years that investments in technology do not predict profitability or growth. Longitudinal research reported by Joyce, Nohria, and Roberson in *What (Really) Works* (2003) reports "no correlation between a company's investment in technology and its total return to shareholders" (p. 7). All of these, and other, arguments were reinforced in Nickolas Carr's (2003) famous article published in the *Harvard Business Review* with the provocative title: "IT Doesn't Matter." Carr is convinced that technology's impact has run its course, that the technology playing field is now level (Carr, 2003, 2004).

Should we believe that computing and communications technology bring little to the competitive table, that the billions and billions companies spend on hardware, software, and technology services every year are somehow misspent? Of course not—still want to disconnect everyone from their digital toys?

There are at least two sides to the value-of-IT coin. The first is about the total dependency that 21st century companies have on IT. The second is about specific relationships among technology investments, profitability, and market share. The dependency argument is solid: no one can argue that 21st century companies do not need IT. The technology-to-profitability argument is now evidence based: in response to the Strassmann/Carr wing, there is research by Mithas, Tafti, Bardhan, and Goh (2012) that finds that "investment companies make in information technology increase profitability more than investments in advertising and R&D" (p. 1).

Arguments that IT no longer matters are ridiculously flawed. In fact, we are confusing several healthy trends with what some see as declining influence. For example, there is no question that laptops and routers are commodities; even many services, like legacy systems maintenance and data center management, have, and absolutely should, become fully commoditized. Are laptops, tablets, and servers "strategic?" No. *But if we botch the acquisition of these devices or fail to adhere to sound management practices like security, they become tactical and strategic liabilities.* Far from being irrelevant, they are actually tactically and strategically necessary.

Another misinterpreted trend is the increase in discipline used to acquire, deploy, and manage technology. We are much more sophisticated about the use of business cases, total-cost-of-ownership (TCO) models, return-on-investment (ROI) calculations, and project management best practices than we were a decade ago. Put another way, the acquisition and management of technology has become routine, no longer the politicized, ad hoc process it once was. Does this mean that it is no longer important? I would argue that our ability to more skillfully acquire and manage IT is an indicator of maturity, not unimportance (Andriole, 2009a,b,c, 2010, 2011, 2012a,b).

Another trend that seems to confuse the "technology does not matter" crowd is our willingness to outsource technology. Companies are reevaluating their sourcing strategies and have lengthened the list of potential candidates for partial and full outsourcing. Some of these include help desk support, programming, and applications maintenance. If we extend this trend it is likely that we will see a lot more hosting of even the largest applications, like enterprise resource planning (ERP) applications, that companies will increasingly rent (to avoid massive implementation costs and ongoing support problems). But does this trend spell the end of IT? Hardly. Outsourcing trends dovetail perfectly with commoditization trends.

Companies have correctly discovered that they do not need to develop core competencies maintaining laptops or supporting Microsoft Office—and why should they? This kind of support should be left to specialists who can offer economies of scale, reliability, and cost-effectiveness. Companies that build and maintain "Centers of Excellence" in the in-house acquisition/deployment/support of operational technology are way, way out of step with procurement trends in the industry. Why would a company of 5,000 global employees spend money to keep Microsoft Office, SAP, or Oracle CRM "up and running" when there are countless vendors who will do it all for them, and for a whole lot less money? Why would a company of 100 employees buy servers, software, and IT gurus? Back in the day—way back in the 1990s—this may have made some sense, but not in the 21st century.

The real story here is not commoditization, discipline, or outsourcing, but the separation of technology into operational and strategic layers—and now, the ready technology layer. Operational technology is what is becoming commoditized; strategic technology is alive and well, and still very much a competitive differentiator. It is even possible to argue that since operational technology has been commoditized, we are now finally ready to strategically leverage technology. Ready technology is fast, cheap, and powerful technology that can amplify operational *and* strategic technology—*and* operational and strategic business processes.

Operational technology enables current and ready business models and processes in well-defined, predictable ways. Hardware price/performance ratios are perhaps the most obvious example of this trend, but there are others including what we are willing to pay for programming services (here and abroad). We now expect companies to excel in the acquisition, deployment, and management of operational technology. We expect them to know what they are doing here—recognizing that mistakes can be extremely costly and even threaten a company's position in the marketplace. Far from being irrelevant, given the size of our technology budgets and our dependency on technology, it is essential that we get the operational layer right. Many companies are very good at it; some companies are horrible. There is huge opportunity—and risk—here: try telling a chief executive officer (CEO) that a botched $100 million ERP project does not matter. Even more relevant to the ready argument is the probability of success of enterprise technology projects: more than half of them fail, so why attempt something that is more likely to fail than succeed.[*]

Strategic technology is the result of creative business technology thinking where, for example, WalMart streamlines its supply chain, Starbucks (and lots of others) offers wireless access to the Web to its retail customers (to keep them inside their stores spending money), and Vanguard leverages its Web site to dramatically improve financial customer service.

---

[*] The data here are downright scary. The Standish Group actually reported that only 16% of software projects succeed (http://kinzz.com/resources/articles/91-project-failures-rise-study-shows). Robbins-Gioia reported that 51% of all ERP projects fail (https://www.google.com/searc?q=robbins+gioia+ppt&ie=utf-8&oe-utf-8&aq-t&rls=org.mozilla:en-US:official&client=firefox-a&channel+sb), and KPMG reported that 61% of technology projects fail to deliver business value (http://tvnz.co.nz/business-news/most-businesses-experience-project-failure-3948434).

There is no limit to how strategic the business technology relationship can be. The exploitation of strategic technology, like customer relationship management (CRM) and its personalization and customization cousins, is dependent upon solid operational technology. The same is true of wireless communications, automation, and dynamic pricing.

Strategic technology is liberated by operational technology. How much time did we spend putting out operational brushfires in the 1980s and 1990s? Was there any time left to think strategically? A lot of basic hardware and software just did not work that well back then, but now technology is reliable and cheap—and now there is finally time to strategically leverage IT—so long as the distinction between operational and strategic technology is well understood. Marching orders?—*solid operational technology that enables creative strategic technology.* If we get this relationship right, technology can contribute directly to efficiency, profitability, and growth.

We are way past the debate about the value of technology. Those who cling to the idea that "IT does not matter" are many of the same people who turned in their cell phones, tablets, and PCs a while ago—if they ever actually used them to solve business problems in the first place. The distinctions among operational and strategic technology are important: both technologies matter more today, and going forward, than they ever did. Our dependency on technology is growing every day and has been for decades. *We are dependent on operational technology, strategic technology, and now ready technology, even if you do not fully understand the dependency or its fundamental importance to corporate survival. Imagine "missing" eBusiness, mobile computing, analytics, or social media.*

Ready technology is a new category of information technology (IT). As Figure I.1 suggests, ready technology sits between, and contributes to, operational and strategic technology.

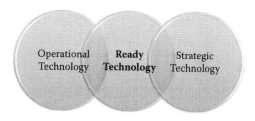

Figure I.1   The range of technologies.

Operational technology can be "ready"; strategic technology can be "ready." Ready technology is technology that is quickly and cheaply deployable. Ready technology is technology that is achieved at a level of maturity that makes it operationally or strategically ready for business.

Operational technology includes infrastructure basics, as Figure I.2 suggests.

Strategic technology is more outward facing, as suggested below (Figure I.3). Where operational technology keeps the lights on, strategic technology sets the corporate agenda. Strategic technology is all about technology-enabled processes, applications, and analytics. It is also about innovation. It is customer defining and customer facing. It is also where technology-enabled (operational and strategic) competitive advantage lives.

Figure I.2 Operational technology.

Figure I.3 Strategic technology.

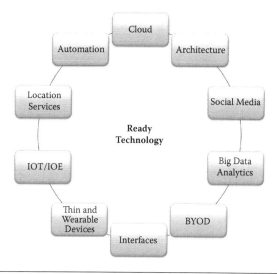

Figure I.4 Ready technology.

Ready technology can be transformative or just part of the "normal" innovation process. The keys are speed and cost. Ready technology *today*—it will certainly change—looks like as shown in Figure I.4.

This book focuses on *ready technology* and the processes by which it is tracked, vetted, piloted, measured, and deployed.

It is a primer *and* a handbook. It is descriptive *and* prescriptive. Figure I.5 provides the road map.

The book is—like the approach and technologies I describe— shovel ready. Hopefully, the arguments influence how we think about technology adoption and enable us to exploit new technologies immediately and effectively.

A methodology for achieving this objective is presented. Examples are discussed.

Everyone can do "IT" this way.

Why focus on "ready" technologies? Why are things so different today than they were five or ten years ago?

There are at least five reasons:

- The pace of digital technology change has dramatically accelerated: fueled by Moore's Law, consumerization, globalization, and a path-to-personal-wealth-creation that increasingly rewards technology entrepreneurs; digital technology is advancing at an unprecedented rate.

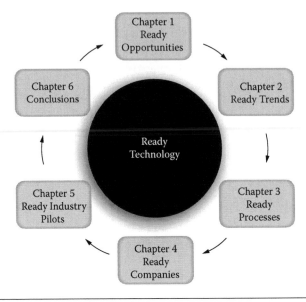

Figure I.5 The organization of *ready technology.*

- The cumulative impact of integrated technology solutions is rapidly expanding: integration and interoperability among technologies is rapidly growing, enabling rapid deployment through internally or externally enabled deployment; software architectures decreasingly require operation on but one device, operating system, and so on—software now travels across networks and devices.

- The ease of deploying ready technologies out of the gate is growing (principally through early maturity and cloud delivery): rather than build data centers, deploy enterprise software applications, and hire huge teams, companies of all sizes can rapidly pilot and deploy ready technologies with little or no initial cost via XaaS delivery models.

- The cost of deploying ready technologies has fallen significantly and shows every sign of falling even more through commoditization and increasingly favorable hardware and software price/performance ratios.

- Companies understand that their ability to compete is tied directly to their ability to leverage digital technology generally and individual technologies specifically: the role that IT plays in every aspect of business is increasing dramatically.

Given these reasons, companies should take six steps:

- Aggressively and Continuously Track Technology Trends
- Optimally Organize to Exploit the Best, and Jettison the Worst, Ready Technologies
- Continuously and Immediately Conduct Ready Technology Pilots
- Rapidly Prioritize, Fund, and Deploy Ready Technologies
- Measure the TCO and ROI of Ready Technology Deployments
- Continuously Repeat the Steps

This book describes the ready technology adoption process in enough detail to allow everyone to immediately and continuously exploit ready technologies.

If I achieve my goals, you will change your perspective on the technology adoption process and come to appreciate just how instantly impactful seemingly brand new technology and technology delivery models can be. But to do all this you will need to reexamine your technology adoption policies and processes. In all likelihood, you will have to significantly modify these policies and processes. Put another way, the real challenge to the full exploitation of ready technologies is the status quo and those who defend things "the way they are—and have always been."

One specific goal is to commit requirements analysis heresy. While I was one of the major advocates of the "requirements-first/technology-second" approach to technology deployment, I have come full circle. I now believe that while the old requirements mantra still applies, there is a whole lot of *technology-driven requirements discovery* that we all need to pursue. Years ago it was expensive and risky to adopt technology on the early side. Today, it is fast, easy, and cheap. That is new and potentially very impactful.

About the Author

Stephen J. Andriole is the Thomas G. Labrecque Professor of Business Technology at Villanova University, Pennsylvania, where he teaches and conducts applied research in business technology management. He is formerly a professor of Information Systems and Electrical and Computer Engineering at Drexel University, Philadelphia, Pennsylvania, and the George Mason Institute Professor of the Department of Information Systems and Systems Engineering at George Mason University, Fairfax, Virginia. Dr. Andriole was the director of the Cybernetics Technology Office of the Defense Advanced Research Projects Agency (DARPA). He was also the chief technology officer and senior vice president of Safeguard Scientifics, Inc., and the chief technology officer and senior vice president for Technology Strategy at Cigna Corporation (Philadelphia, Pennsylvania and Bloomfield, Connecticut).

Some of Dr. Andriole's books include *Interactive Computer-Based Systems Design and Development* (Petrocelli Books, 1983); *Microcomputer Decision Support Systems* (QED Information Sciences, 1985); *Applications in Artificial Intelligence* (Petrocelli Books, 1986); *Information System Design Principles for the 90s* (AFCEA International Press, 1990); *Sourcebook of Applied Artificial Intelligence* (McGraw-Hill, 1992); *Cognitive Systems Engineering* (coauthored with Len Adelman) on user interface technology (Lawrence Erlbaum Associates, 1995); *Managing Systems Requirements Methods, Tools and Cases* (McGraw-Hill, 1996); *The 2nd Digital Revolution* (IGI Press, 2005); *Technology Due Diligence* (IGI Press, 2009); *Best Practices in Business Technology Management* (Auerbach, 2009); and *IT's All About the People* (Auerbach, 2011). He is also the coauthor of *Social Business Intelligence* (Ascendigm Press, 2013) and *Avoiding #Fail* (Ascendigm Press, 2013).

Dr. Andriole has published articles in the *Cutter IT Journal, Software Development, IEEE Software,* the *Communications of the ACM,* the *Communications of the AIS, IEEE IT Professional,* and the *Journal of Information Technology Research,* among other academic and practitioner journals. His *IT's All About the People* won the fourth spot for Best Business Technology Books for 2011 by *CIO Insight* magazine.

For more information about Dr. Andriole's career, please visit: http://www.andriole.com.

1

READY OPPORTUNITIES

When I was Cigna's (NYSE: CI) chief technology officer (CTO), Cigna underinvested in technology. I tried to get more money— especially strategic money—into the technology budget, but I failed. Here is what I wrote about Cigna's technology investment philosophy (Andriole, 2005):

> In the 1990s I sat in the office of a CEO of a Fortune 100 company. He was not happy about the annual technology bill. Back then—and for decades before—technology was tactical. He said something about technology being his last unmanaged expense. I gave him a list of ten things we should do to improve the cost-effectiveness of our technology investments; he told me to come back when there were only three things on the list. There was no appetite for long discussions about what was wrong— or right—with technology, and there was an expectation that technology expenses could be reduced by focusing on the top three problems.
>
> The conversation was anything but strategic. It was about technology as real estate, or technology as furniture, something we had to have, a necessary evil, a cost incurred to support the transactions that made us money. The business itself was never discussed. It was almost as if technology existed independently of business models and processes.

Cigna's senior management team did not "believe" in operational *or* strategic technology; they did not see technology investments as a path to increased revenue or profitability. They saw technology as a cost center that had to be managed, or more accurately, reduced. They looked for ways to avoid technology investments. I remember walking out of the chief executive officer's (CEO's) office wondering what he was going to do to the technology budget. (One day he suggested we shut e-mail down to save money and increase productivity.) There is more: while just about everyone was investing in the Internet in the late 1990s with new transactional business models defined around ubiquitous connectivity, a very senior Cigna executive declared during a corporate off-site that the Internet was a "fad that would be gone in a couple of years." (Quite a few of us were beyond stunned by the proclamation; I remember us looking at each other in disbelief and, well, a little fear: "now what?" we wondered. As CTO, I felt that my mission was to upgrade the company's technology platform and business models, but when a senior executive declares that the Internet would not be part of the future platform (on top of the general "technology-is-a-cost-center" perspective), well, I felt like I did not have much of a future at the company. In fact, I resigned less than a year later.

Was Cigna an aberration? Remember that the traditional insurance industry is notoriously technophobic: many of the technology-driven advances in the industry came from online start-ups like Insweb (http://www.insweb.com), SelectQuote (http://www.selectquote.com), and eHealth (http://www.ehealthinsurance.com). There were many companies—not just Cigna—in the 20th century that saw technology strictly as cost centers that threatened earnings before interest, depreciation, and amortization (EBIDA) every time their chief information officers (CIOs) uttered the word "upgrade." At the same time, there were lots of companies (in other industries) that began a deliberate pivot from technology as cost center to technology as profit center, often because of the eBusiness opportunities that the Internet "fad" created.

After Cigna, I found myself at Safeguard Scientifics (NYSE: SFE), a technology holding and operating company, where the corporate mission was identifying technology trends and investing in the ones with the most promise. We made big bets on technologies, taking many companies public in just a few years. Yes, it was the dot.com bubble—the mission was to find the technologies most likely to change the world and place significant bets on their potential. We were sometimes very wrong, but sometimes *very right*: one of the companies we took public, the Internet Capital Group (that still exists today), enjoyed a $50 billion market cap shortly after its initial public offering (IPO). The rules were clear: identify technology trends, convert the trends into viable business models, and monetize them as quickly as possible. Not all of the technologies were ready for deployment; many were immature and unproven. Safeguard's modus operandi was (Internet) speed regardless of demonstrated capability. The bets were about potential.

Fast forward to the early 21st century: the pace of technology change, the cumulative effect of technology solutions, and the ease of deploying new technologies has made Safeguard's mission everyone's mission. Companies can now directly acquire and deploy ready technologies. *In fact, this is the new technology adoption modus operandi.*

Not so many years ago companies could be late adopters of powerful digital technologies. When I was at Cigna, we looked at enterprise resource planning (ERP), network and systems management, and Internet technologies without urgency (but with obvious financial and management constraints), and ultimately declined to spend significant money in these areas. In the 20th century, companies could wait until their industries and competitors fully vetted specific technologies before investing in even the most tried-and-true ones. In the 1990s, companies loved to remind technophiles that they deliberately avoided "bleeding edge" technologies. Technophobes believed that investing too early was indulgent and reckless. Many executives wore their late technology adoption strategies as badges of corporate honor. Some of them were actually right about waiting, but many others preferred waiting because it provided a terrific excuse to reduce existing—or avoid new—technology expenses.

But spotting your competition a technology lead of a year or two today, *given how powerful new technologies are out of the gate,* is dangerous. Many new technologies are easily ready for pilot assessments if not full-enterprise deployment.

The Ready Backdrop

There are five reasons why things are different today:

- The pace of digital technology change has dramatically accelerated: fueled by Moore's Law, consumerization, globalization, and a path to personal wealth creation that increasingly rewards technology entrepreneurs; digital technology is advancing at an unprecedented rate.
- The cumulative impact of integrated technology solutions is rapidly expanding: integration and interoperability among technologies is rapidly growing, enabling rapid deployment through internally or externally enabled deployment; software

architectures decreasingly require operation on but one device, operating system, and so on; and software now travels across networks and devices.

- The ease of deploying ready technologies out of the gate is growing (principally through early maturity and cloud delivery): rather than building data centers, deploying enterprise software applications, and hiring huge teams, companies of all sizes can rapidly pilot and deploy ready technologies with little or no initial cost via XaaS delivery models.
- The cost of deploying ready technologies has fallen significantly and shows every sign of falling even more through commoditization and increasingly favorable hardware and software price/performance ratios.
- Companies understand that their ability to compete is tied directly to their ability to leverage digital technology generally and individual technologies specifically: the role that information technology plays in every aspect of business is dramatically increasing in importance.

Given these reasons, companies should take six steps:

- Aggressively and Continuously Track Technology Trends
- Optimally Organize to Exploit the Best—and Jettison the Worst—Ready Technologies
- Continuously and Immediately Conduct Ready Technology Pilots
- Rapidly Prioritize, Fund, and Deploy Ready Technologies
- Measure the Total Cost of Ownership (TCO) and Return on Investment (ROI) of Ready Technology Deployments
- Continuously Repeat the Process

Not only should companies track technology trends, but they need to determine as quickly as possible through well-structured technology pilots which technologies will help them the most. Then they must immediately deploy the technologies. Delay puts companies at competitive risk.

For example, how many companies deployed *iPads* immediately after they were introduced? Thousands were sold before corporate information technology (IT) groups could declare them "nonstandard" and unsecure. The same early adopters immediately found programmers to write iPad software applications that made their marketing teams more agile. Corporate IT chased them around and around, but at the end of the day everyone got to keep their iPads and IT declared them "safe"—*well after their deployment*. Fast, creative deployments legitimized iPads as solutions to an array of well-known *and yet to be discovered* problems. Specifically, iPad applications can be built in weeks and months, not years—and for $25,000 to $50,000 (not $250,000 to $500,000, or much more, the typical price large consultancies charge to write custom applications). iPads can replace laptops for many managers and executives, especially those who *react* (to the work of others) versus those who *create* (reports, spreadsheets, and presentations). iPads consume less power. iPads are cool. At the end of the day, they save money, make money, and improve services. Their deployment was instant—and impactful. Very few of us took the position that the first iPad was probably half-baked and that it made sense to wait for the iPad 2, 3, or 4. *Instead, they grabbed as many as they could grab and immediately began the solutions discovery process.*

Another example is *social media*. How many companies are "listening" to what their customers, and competitors, are saying about them? Once it was possible to listen to all flavors of social conversations, companies quickly found listening partners (ListenLogic/Akuda Labs, Radian6 [now part of salesforce.com], Crimson Hexagon, etc.) and started mining social data about what their customers liked and disliked about their products and services (and the products and services of their competitors). *There was no need for corporate IT to get involved.* Multiple corporate functions—marketing, risk management, brand management, competitor intelligence—all directly availed themselves of "social business intelligence." Brand managers did not wait for the listening technology to further mature or for the listening process to be defined. They just signed listening contracts and began to extract value from the social conversation. Many of these contracts were with listening vendors who deliver their services in the cloud.

Bring your own device (*BYOD*) is yet another example. The BYOD-to-work delivery model gained momentum immediately after it was described by industry gurus, creative companies, and even a few academics. Countless companies launched pilots to determine the strengths and weaknesses of the delivery model even before anyone gave the model a name. The idea is simple enough. Since employees have their favorite machines and software applications—and are most productive when they use "personal technology"—and since many companies would love to reduce and eventually eliminate the expensive employee technology benefit, pilots were launched first under the corporate radar and then with great fanfare. BYOD is now a formal movement led by chief financial officers (CFOs), CIOs, and CEOs who like the idea of letting people use whatever technology they want, especially if it reduces technology costs.

iPads, social media, and BYOD are instantly deployed. All were new technologies with new technology delivery models, but all were "ready" for immediate deployment. Technology has become a game changer. Not since the Internet became a transaction platform in the mid-to-late 1990s have we seen such transformative technology.

Except this time it is pervasive.

It is not a platform, or some new access device, or some "killer app," it is all of these things and more. Failing to understand the new rules around technology adoption could be fatal. Today's new technologies are not "disruptive," they are immediately transformative. This is not about "crossing the chasm" or solving the "innovator's dilemma." Both of those arguments were interesting in the 20th century but are obsolete today. Companies do not have years to pursue the old "people/process/technology" adoption strategy. They do not have years, or even months, to deliberate about the depth or trajectory of "disruptive technologies" or the difficulty of "crossing the chasm." Ready technology adoption is related to, but different from, the adoption "chasm" described by Geoffrey A. Moore (1991). Moore argues that there is a chasm between early adopters and the early majority that must be managed by high-tech marketers. "Ready" is quite different from the "chasm," because ready technology is low cost and low risk. Ready is not a conundrum that requires specialized marketing.

Companies that want to compete should rethink the way they define, vet, and deploy digital technology. They must become immediate, continuous adopters of ready technologies. Traditional paths to technology adoption are now obsolete. The above examples suggest that consumerization and other technology development/deployment forces are already at work flipping the technology adoption model on its head. In the 20th century, we started with business requirements and then looked to technology to satisfy them. Remember all of the seminars, books, and articles on "requirements engineering," "requirements management," and "business technology alignment?"

Remember when (some saw) iPads were solutions in search of problems? Countless technology and financial pundits wondered publicly just what people would do with iPads (and tablets generally). Many suggested that iPads would be expensive toys with much less functionality than average laptops. Others predicted Apple's demise. No one had a good description of the requirements iPads would satisfy or the processes that tablets would redefine. So without any advance requirements analyses, they were aggressively imported, with no specific mission, into company after company. *iPads were "discovered" in real time. The iPad adoption process—the technology adoption life cycle at work—consisted of "let's buy some and see what they can do."*

Similarly, social media listening was ready, discoverable technology. Brand managers and market researchers realized that the social conversation was huge and the source of insights that even the largest focus group or survey could not possibly generate. So they started listening. Then they listened some more. They hired multiple listening partners. They mined the conversations the same way "barefoot empiricists" search for statistical correlations, even if no one's ever imagined the correlations. They just listened and mined. *They had no idea what they would discover.*

What about BYOD? Again, the technology adoption life cycle was flipped on its head. Corporate IT seldom recommended BYOD. Employees and budget busters were the unlikely bedfellows that drove the pilots that drove early adoption. *Here again the adoption process was "let's try it and see what happens."* Companies discovered that some of their infrastructures were not BYOD ready, that it actually increased costs, and that (especially) new employees absolutely loved BYOD. Some discovered that BYOD helped them recruit and retain younger employees and that technology costs actually fell.

All sorts of discoveries are made every time a company decides to deploy a new technology or technology delivery model.

Safe is no longer slow.

What are some of today's ready technologies?

There is no shortage of lists, insights, and opinions. Figure 1.1 presents a picture (based on the analysis of the research and

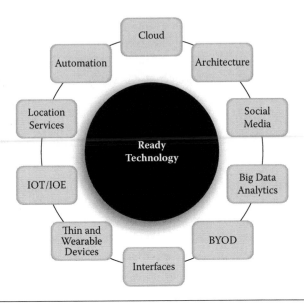

Figure 1.1   Ready technology.

development [R&D] budgets of technology vendors, where the venture capital industry is placing its bets, how *Wall Street* defines forward value, and close collaboration with technology research organizations, pundits, and bloggers). Note that investments in these technologies is brisk, and note that the investments are not to make the technologies viable but to extend their applicability to known and unknown problems and opportunities.

So how should the list convert into immediate pilots and rapid deployments? What can you do with the 10 technology clusters? *What are the ready pilots you can launch tomorrow?*

Ready Pilots

Look at the 10 technology clusters one at a time and suggest what you can do to exploit their capabilities.

Begin with cloud computing.

One of the major strengths of *cloud computing* is the freedom it provides companies to think operationally and strategically about how they want to leverage digital technology. Instead of worrying about network latency and server maintenance, business technology professionals can focus on innovation, sales, and marketing, among other revenue-generating activities (within and beyond the cloud). Another strength is flexibility. Picking from a menu is easier than designing one and then delivering the food. Scalability is often just a phone call, e-mail, or alert away. The freedom from software maintenance, denial-of-service attacks, software version control, viruses, backup and recovery, and other operational headaches is provided by cloud computing (assuming your cloud provider is competent, of course).

It is essential that companies quickly define, quantify, and assess cloud delivery performance metrics. In addition to standard quantitative metrics are the qualitative ones that measure the overall effectiveness of a new delivery model. Perceptions are important, though not deal breakers, and quantitative performance metrics that answer the most obvious questions about availability, scalability, security, reliability, and the like are essential to developing a solid business case for cloud computing. Metrics are industry and company specific. The objective ones should address impact, risk, and cost. Key to the adoption or rejection of cloud computing is continuous performance assessment. While early metrics may look good, later ones may not. A long view is necessary to accurately measure the impact of cloud computing: companies should not be too quick to enter or leave the cloud. Note, however, that "long" here does not mean years: you should be able to understand the strengths/weaknesses/opportunities/threats (SWOT) of cloud computing in several months.

Cloud delivery is one of the pillars of ready technology. The fast and cheap aspect of ready technology piloting and deployment is more often than not enabled by cloud delivery. It is safe to say that without cloud delivery, ready technology would not be nearly as important as it is today. *Cloud delivery makes many ready technologies ready.*

Here are some cloud activities to consider:

- Simultaneously launch infrastructure, applications, and development cloud pilots: select a candidate infrastructure service, a significant application, and a development project to "test" the cloud's security, reliability, and scalability.
- Engage your internal and external auditors with a set of cloud standards that work for your industry, especially if that industry is a highly regulated industry that requires "validated" technology: develop an internal cloud policy.

- Adopt and deploy accordingly: develop a long-term cloud strategy informed by diagnostic cloud service-level agreements (SLAs).

Distributed architectures, application programming interfaces (APIs), and software components are yielding rapid-active versus slow-passive software design. Passive design is what software engineers have practiced for decades: someone identifies "requirements" and then some others code functionality into inflexible software applications. Everything is fine until a new requirement emerges and changes must be made. Enhanced functionality comes in the form of releases with new features released and supported by the creator of the software— on the creator's schedule. Instead of rigid, embedded processes, active software architectures enable the addition or subtraction of functionality through component architectures and APIs that will grow increasingly flexible and available from a variety of sources including the original authors of the software and all kinds of software mercenaries. Open-source APIs will make it possible to reengineer functional designs in near real time. Software will be designed in interoperable pieces, not monolithic structures. APIs and other components will enable functional interoperability, extensibility, and adaptability. The integration of disparate cloud delivery technologies is also part of the trend toward architecture compatibility, which is extremely important to the adoption of ready technology.

It is impossible to discuss where software will come from without examining "app stores." The number of applications appearing monthly is staggering. But more significantly, app stores represent a whole new software development and distribution channel. Even more stunning are the prices of the software applications at these stores. Countless robust business applications sell for way under $50. Some cost less than $10. What this means for all of us is a whole new way to define software applications and whole new ways to acquire them at unheard of price points, especially given what corporate software buyers are used to paying.

Here is what can be done immediately:

- Track app store download trends and measure the impact of cheap apps across a set of business value-derived performance metrics: test them weekly.

- Track mashup/API releases and measure the impact of mashups across performance metrics and negative metrics, like enterprise software licensing and third-party application development trends: build an API repository and conduct continuous in-house tests of the power of open APIs for mashup application development and interoperability.
- Track open-source adoption trends across small, medium, and large businesses, especially with reference to how open-source software (OSS) is replacing proprietary software: deploy open-source software like OpenOffice and Hadoop/MapReduce (for big data analyses).
- Track the adoption of software-as-a-service (SaaS) delivery models and measure the impact on speed, agility, and the cost of all of the on-demand/pay-by-the-drink software delivery models: open multiple accounts immediately and test them for cost, access, security, and impact.

Social media is everywhere. *Social business intelligence* is the goal. The intersection of traditional structured data (about customers, products, and sales) and unstructured social data (from Facebook, Twitter, YouTube, forums, and blogs) represents opportunities for next-generation business intelligence and predictive analytics. The billions of posts, tweets, and blogs every month represent the richest communications and collaboration channel in history. Ready companies are developing formal, and permanent, social media listening and analysis strategies as we speak. It is important to explore the options and weigh the results against a set of listening/analysis/engagement goals (which, ideally, are derived from an explicit social media strategy).

So given all of this, what is social media really good for? How about the following, for starters:

- Market Research
- Brand Management
- Competitive Intelligence
- Product Innovation and Life Cycle Management
- Customer Service
- Threat Tracking
- Risk Management

Here are some ready social business intelligence pilots:

- Open at least one account, immediately, with a social media listening/engagement vendor and test a set of hypotheses about internal and external social business intelligence: sign some listening/engagement contracts designed to test a variety of listening/engagement methods, tools, and techniques.
- Listen to what your employees, customers, and suppliers are saying about your company, its products and services, competitors, and the industry: profile the style and content of the discussion and your company's place in that discussion; identify engagement actions/reactions your company should undertake.
- Determine what you need to know about the social conversation to improve customer service, innovation, and brand management: develop a social media deployment strategy.

The *real-time big data analytics* challenge is real and growing. "Data" are no longer owned by the enterprise. They are created by everyone: vendors, customers, suppliers, partners, managers, executives, strangers, bloggers, and vagabonds, among anyone else who would like to offer insights, solve problems, or buy things.

The end-game is simple: real-time descriptive, explanatory, predictive, and prescriptive data, information, and knowledge about internal and external processes and performance. But there are challenges. The amount of data streaming into companies today is huge and growing. The "big data" problem is very real. Big data analysis will become the next must-have competency as the volume of digital content grows to 2.7 zettabytes (ZB), up 48% from 2011. Over 90% of this information is unstructured (images, MP3 files, videos, and social media)—full of rich information but difficult to profile and analyze (see Frank Gens, IDC Predictions 2012: Competing for 2020, December 1, 2011).

The power of analytics is clear: the more descriptive, explanatory, predictive, and prescriptive insight a company has, the better its operational and strategic performance will be. The ability to observe and tune operations and strategy, especially in real time, is essential to competitive positioning and growth. Analytics is awareness and engagement. Companies that ignore analytics will significantly weaken their ability to compete.

Here are some real-time big data analytics pilots:

- Determine the range of social/sensor/transaction big data at your company: immediately profile the range of big data constraints and opportunities.
- Install Hadoop (and other big data) applications to determine the potential for structured and unstructured data analytics: implement big data platforms (and/or big data extensions from your existing database management platforms) designed to collect, profile, and analyze structured and unstructured big data; "solve" some selected real-time big data problems with off-the-shelf open-source big data platforms.
- Measure: deploy as appropriate.

BYOD is already at work. We are all familiar with the model. Employees, suppliers, and partners are encouraged to use whatever digital devices they prefer while working in, or interacting with, your company. Some believe that the BYOD movement is about reducing corporate technology expenses, while others believe that happy employees/suppliers/partners are productive employees/suppliers/partners. It is a fast-moving trend that is uncovering a lot of issues that companies and their technology providers are quickly addressing.

BYOD will continue to define device adoption—perhaps forever. As vendors produce more and more feature-rich, celebrity-endorsed devices, professionals will adopt more and more consumer devices, regardless of what their corporate IT people tell them they can and cannot do.

The work here includes the following:

- Immediate, multiple BYOD pilots of a meaningful number of employees around quantitative TCO/ROI performance metrics: measure/adopt/deploy.
- Establish a policy around BYOD designed to institutionalize the identification and integration of new devices: create a proactive policy designed to exploit the best and most popular new devices.

The *interfaces* we use to interact with hardware and software of all kinds are changing. Speech input is becoming more capable, and other interface technology like gesture control is also gaining momentum.

Displays are becoming more interactive and intuitive: "visualization" was impressive in the 1990s, and today it is essential and intelligent. Biometrics are now, after many years, moving to mainstream. While there were deployments of biometric technology in selected industries and for specific purposes, the iPhone has finally consumerized biometric authentication. Facial recognition technology (and other biometric interfaces) is also advancing at a rapid pace. Such technology will facilitate access to, and other "controls" of, devices, processes, and transactions.

The way we interact with hardware and software is directly linked to productivity. Interface technology is about convenience and performance. Advanced interface technology is ready for adoption.

The work here includes the following:

- Assess the range of current interface technology at your company (and your home): measure the cost-effectiveness of the current suite.
- Pilot new interface technology to determine its TCO/ROI: focus specifically on speech, biometrics, and gesture control.

Thin and wearable is here. Most of us access the Internet with a *"thin" device*. Increasingly these devices are *on* or even *in* us. While we still use desktops and laptops, increasingly we use tablets, smartphones, and other thin clients to access local area networks, wide area networks, virtual private networks, the Internet, hosted applications on these networks, as well as applications that run locally on (some of) the devices. The economics are so compelling for thin clients that we can expect the "fat" corporate PC and the venerable laptop to go the way of employer-provided health insurance: by 2017 less than half of the largest enterprises will still provide free computers with support to their employees. The other half will provide low-cost, thin clients (smartphone, tablets, etc.) or offer a "technology credit" (as part of the growing BYOD trend).

Just as exciting are the wearables that are appearing with increasing frequency. Google Glass, Apple's iWatch, Plantronics' Bluetooth headsets, among countless do-it-yourself (DIY)-enabling devices, are changing the way we search, navigate, transact, and live. Chips can be implanted (inside of us; inside of anything) for all sorts of activities, and security and connectivity will be enabled by stomach-acid-activated capsules we swallow, as appropriate.

Here are the pilots:

- Track the thin/wearable trends closely: assign a team to identify and assess opportunities in thin/wearable ready technology deployment.
- Acquire, deploy, and assess thin/wearable technology: conduct TCO and ROI analyses.

The Internet of Things (IOT) and the Internet of Everything (IOE) will change just about everything we think we know and do about mobility, search, transaction processing, and even personal relationship management. Fueling all this is the fact that within a few years the vast majority of Internet protocol (IP) traffic will be driven by wireless devices.

The explosion of IP "identity cards" for literally everything will enable business models and processes that assume integration and continuity. The old term, "pervasive computing," is now actualized.

It will also enable personal business models and processes and the intersection of business and personal models and processes. Imagine when everything is addressable, accessible, and manipulable. Imagine when we can talk to and connect everything and every person on the planet. IOT/IOE is an infrastructure technology that will enable all sorts of imagined and unimagined activities. The more it spreads, the more activities it will support.

Here are some IOT/IOE pilots:

- Assign a team to track IOT/IOE trends in your industry: develop a rolling list of IOT/IOE-inspired opportunities.
- Implement IOT/IOE-enabled activities, processes, and transactions: test and measure impact.

Location awareness fundamentally alters business processes across multiple functional areas, but especially in sales and marketing. Enabled by GPS (and other) technology, retailers can track customers and tempt them with real-time and other offers. But these are only a few of the services that location awareness enables.

The key is to define location-based services and discover the requirements that the technology can satisfy. For example, retailers have a clear, vested interest in knowing where their customers physically are. They need to know the movement patterns of their customers, and they need to correlate locations with a variety of attributes such as time of day, age, gender, wealth, and race, among other variables. The next step is to infer from that data precisely how to engage that customer with just the right communications and offers. Location awareness thus enables customer analytics.

The major consumer location-based platforms include Yelp, Neer, Loopt, SCVNGR, Gowalla, and Foursquare. These platforms enable a variety of activities and transactions and link to other social media sites to enable an "experience" that is both fun and monetizable. Companies have developed their own location-aware applications that employees, suppliers, and customers can download onto their laptops, smartphones, and tablets—*all of their mobile devices.*

Historical location data can provide insight into the travels of customers, suppliers, partners, and employees. Companies need to prepare for all the primary and secondary transactions that location awareness enables. Again, analytics is one of the capabilities that location awareness enables.

The power of location-awareness and location-based services is growing. When combined with data about consumer preferences, location-based services enable the real-time correlation of location-based marketing, selling, and service. Companies that touch customers with products and services should avail themselves of location-awareness and location-based services, or find themselves at a competitive disadvantage to those who do. The relationship among analytics, social media, and location awareness is clear and cumulative. When integrated with mobility and cloud computing, the potential is even greater.

Companies should prepare for the collection and analysis of location data over time:

- Enlist one or more of the major location-based service vendors to determine where, how, and with what effect location-based services can enhance your business models and processes, especially those related to customer, employee, and supplier mobility: collect and activate location-based data.
- Launch a location-based, service-based analytics pilot to determine the diagnostic power of reactive and proactive location-based data: measure and deploy.

Intelligent automation is the natural extension of artificial intelligence (AI) and expert systems design and development. It is also about the next generation of applications already appearing in horizontal technology architectures, like network and systems management frameworks, and in vertical applications, like those intended to make customer service representatives more effective. Many of these applications have some level of embedded intelligence.

Intelligent, automated systems will continue to routinize many decision-making processes. Rules about investment, management, resource allocation, and office administration will be embedded in automated applications. It is unlikely that individuals will go onto the Web and execute trivial transactions. Smart support systems will automatically execute hundreds of predefined, "authorized" transactions. There are expert system shells and templates that permit the design and implementation of automated transactions. There are off-the-shelf tools that support automation, though they are not always identified as important business process modeling applications. There are "rules" around processes and transactions that can be automated, as they already are within some (especially) retail transaction processing.

Some pilots here include the following:

- Look for opportunities to leverage intelligent automation; assign a team to assess the potential of intelligent technology across your business processes and models: canvass the intelligent automation/AI landscape—universities, articles, books, and conferences.
- Determine the range of automated opportunities: extend your business model and processes to include intelligent automation; answer the simple question: what can we automate quickly and cheaply?
- Launch selected pilots with tools and shells designed to intelligently automate major and minor business processes; measure TCO/ROI: launch, measure, and deploy.

In the 20th century, technology adoption was a slow, disciplined process. Most companies, CIOs, and business unit executives were skeptical about what "new" technologies could actually deliver.

Companies obviously felt that technology was necessary, but they also believed that technology adoption should be very carefully managed. The horror stories about companies jumping into new technology projects too early or without proper due diligence were more than just urban legends.

Consumerization, cloud delivery, and agile management best practices have changed the technology adoption equation. It is now possible to "fail fast/fail cheap"—a longtime technology adoption goal. Because of the fail-fast/fail-cheap capability, companies can now "discover" requirements and experiment with the power of ready technology with relatively little risk.

Figure 1.2 maps the opportunities. The list of ready technologies in the cells will change over time. The key is to track them, pilot them, and where appropriate, deploy and measure them.

Figure 1.2 also suggests that there are internal and external pilots designed to enhance strategic and tactical performance.

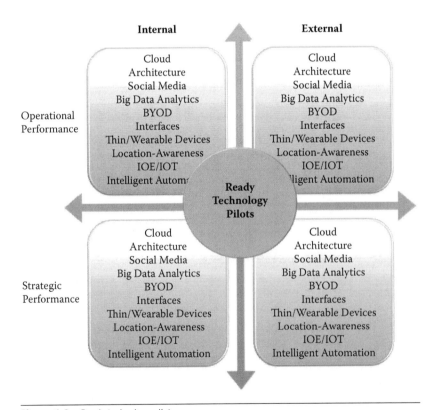

Figure 1.2 Ready technology pilots.

The tracking/piloting/deployment of ready technology is a new core competency. Technology will continue to advance and pilot/deployment delivery will continue to improve. The adoption of ready technology will become a competitive activity that companies will have to pursue. A new set of best practices will develop around ready technology tracking, piloting, and deployment. Agility and competitiveness will redefine themselves around ready technology.

Figure 1.2 is a blueprint. It presents the range of ready technology pilots at this point in time. The range will change over time as new technologies arrive. Note that the pace at which new technologies arrive will not abate. There is every reason to believe that it will accelerate. So the need to find, pilot, and deploy ready technologies will only grow.

2
READY TECHNOLOGY TRENDS

It is hard to imagine anyone handing out heavy Wintel monsters to employees in five years. Devices will get smaller, faster, and smarter—finally killing off the "fat clients" of the 1980s, 1990s, and early 2000s. Wikis, blogs, mashups, social networks, RSS filters, crowdsourcing, virtual worlds, automated pricing, and intelligent supply chains will define the future. Many companies, even the largest ones, will move toward open-source software solutions. Business intelligence (BI) is a strategic investment everyone will make. The era of fixed-location computing is over, and just about everyone is already renting software over the Web. Ultimately, we will all move to the cloud.[*]

How will these and related trends define our technology future?

Figure 2.1 provides perspective.

The range of ready technologies within these trends is formidable. The challenge is to select the ones most likely to quickly and cost-effectively impact business models and processes—that is, find the most ready ones.

Understanding the history and trajectory of technology is important to appreciating its potential. Technologists that have, for example, tracked the evolution of cloud computing can better define its contribution to technology delivery. Understanding "cloud" as initially time-sharing, then distributed computing, then application service providers, and then true plug-and-play provides insights that can be tested in structured pilots.

---

[*] See Luis M. Vaquero, et al., "A Break in the Clouds: Towards a Cloud Definition," *ACM SIGCOMM Computer Communication Review*, Vol. 39, No. 1, January 2009; John Horrigan, "Use of Cloud Computing Applications and Services," Pew Internet and American Life Project, September 12, 2008; San Murugesan, "Cloud Computing: A New Paradigm in IT," *Cutter Business Intelligence Executive Report*, Vol. 9, No. 2, 2009; Ken Orr and Andy Maher, "Here Comes Cloud Computing," *Cutter Consortium Business Technology Trends and Impacts Council Opinion*, Vol. 10, No. 1, 2009.

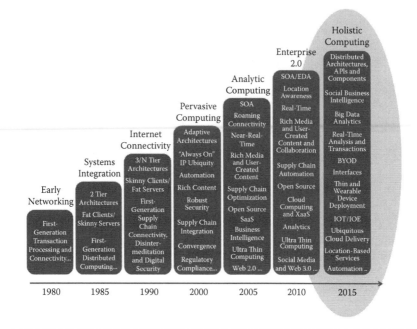

Figure 2.1 Macro technology trends.

The overarching technology themes that deserve our attention and define the range of ready technology opportunities can be aggregated as follows:

- Software for Hire
- Devices/People/Tasks Alignment
- Analytics Here, Now, and Forever
- Respect Social Media
- Innovation/Innovation/More Innovation
- Missions to the Cloud

We discuss them in more detail.

Software for Hire

One thing is for sure: the hammerlock that the big proprietary software vendors have had on the market—even over the big enterprises is over. Their biggest customers are always looking for ways to deliver the same functionality for much less money (and better service). My work with chief information officers (CIOs) and chief technology officers (CTOs) clearly demonstrates that the vast majority of technology buyers believe that software costs way too much. The big software vendors must change their pricing models, open their architectures, and learn to love hosting by themselves and third-party partners if they want to grow. The days of 60% to 70% software profit margins are long gone. The days of controlling customers with hardware architectures, service packs, and poor integration and interoperability are also gone. The number of alternative software applications and the ability to deliver applications cost-effectively through nontraditional channels has fundamentally changed the game. In fact, it is only a matter of time before the major enterprise software vendors cannibalize their own software delivery models to protect their market share: they will persist with the current enterprise licensing models for as long as they can. When the well runs dry, they will move quickly to not only offer new pricing alternatives but claim that they supported alternative pricing all along. Cynical? Not really. Proprietary software vendors have charged as much as they could for their products and services for as long as they could, for decades. Why would they seek ways to charge their customers less? The answer lies in urgency and alternatives: they will adjust their pricing only when they have to; they will offer alternatives when the competition puts a gun to their heads.

Another major change will be active versus passive software design. Passive design is what software engineers have practiced for decades: someone identifies "requirements" and then some others code functionality into inflexible software applications. Everything is fine until a new requirement emerges and changes must be made. SAP (and others) has perfected the "do-IT-my-way" approach to software design: they, as many others, have embedded rigid processes into their applications and declared that the really "smart" users of their software will learn to adapt to the embedded processes versus customizing their near-perfect applications. Company after company deployed SAP (and other enterprise resource planning [ERP]) software and then wrestled with the process changes necessary to optimize the use of the applications. Enhanced functionality comes in the form of releases where the proprietary vendor decides which new features will be released and when they will be released and supported by the supreme creator of the software. In many respects, the embedded rigidity of 20th century proprietary enterprise software applications represents the way we acquired, deployed, and supported technology way back in the day.

As discussed briefly above, instead of a rigid, embedded process, active software architectures enable the addition or subtraction of functionality through component architectures and application programming interfaces (APIs) that will grow increasingly flexible and available from a variety of sources including the original authors of the software and all kinds of software mercenaries. Open-source APIs will make it possible to reengineer functional designs in near real time. Even today we have enough APIs to make business analysts and requirements managers salivate, and every month more are published. Software will be designed in interoperable pieces, not monolithic structures. APIs and other components will enable functional interoperability, extensibility, and adaptability.

All of this enables a new software artifact: the (instant) mashup. Mashups represent the new prototypes, and the new mashup development environments represent what we used to describe as rapid application development (RAD) integrated development environments (IDEs). Mashups are the poor, or impatient, man's applications. While today's mashups are toys, tomorrow's will be sturdy, interoperable, and extensible.

What about open-source software (OSS)? The adoption of OSS will rise. But the real impact will be in the larger open architectures that OSS encourages. More pieces of proprietary software will be built around open standards. The whole service-oriented architecture (SOA) trend relies upon open, reusable, and cataloguable components. For software to truly become a service, it has to open up and be inventoried. Everyone needs to know where it is, what it does, what it costs, and what impact it is likely to have on major and minor business processes. Published metadata about software functionality, applications, and (reusable) components will enable the optimal selection and use of software solutions.

Beyond open architecture are the specific OSS applications that are challenging their proprietary twins. Osalt.com lists the major proprietary software along with its open-source alternatives (http://www. osalt.com). It is amazing how many open-source applications have impressed even the most conservative information technology (IT) buyers over the past five years. OSS is creeping into every layer of the software stack; it is also appearing under its own labels: where no one sees Apace, everyone sees what is happening with Google apps, Google docs, OpenOffice, MySQL, SugarCRM, and Hadoop/MapReduce among countless others.

"Programming," as we have known it for decades, will morph into a variety of skills and competencies (much, probably, to the chagrin of the software engineering community). There will be a set of professionals highly skilled in architecture, APIs, and mashup technology that may well become the requirements-fulfilling front line of transaction processing. Perhaps the best indication of how successful this new set of professionals becomes will be measured in the go-to behavior of their business partners: if the business tilts toward them to satisfy requirements, instead of the traditional systems development life cycle (SDLC) crowd, then "programming" will have morphed to problem solving.

Finally, consider the location of the software we actually use to enable communication, analysis, and transaction processing. Does it sit on your or your provider's server? Does it matter? The movement of data center responsibility from internally serviced centers to centers in the cloud describes the journey that software has taken over the decades, not to mention the journey that pricing has taken over the same period. We see more pay-by-the-drink pricing models, even if the drink only takes a few minutes or seconds.

So where will software applications come from? Just about everywhere. Software design and development will be shared and distributed among software engineers and business analysts using tools and techniques that the industry will provide as part of the ongoing march toward openness and interoperability. The whole notion of releases, upgrades, service packs, and version control will no longer dominate software availability. Waiting for tomorrow's software release to solve today's business problems will occur infrequently as functional alternatives grow in number and capacity. Why wait when you can build a mashup? Or visit an app store?

The big questions, that the tracking suggested below would answer, should focus on what future SDLCs will look like, what software procurement best practices will evolve to, what software acquisition, deployment, and support performance metrics will emerge, and what "software development" will actually mean.

Here is what you should track:

- App store download trends and measure the impact of cheap apps across a set of business value–derived performance metrics
- Mashup/API releases and measure the impact of mashups across performance metrics and negative metrics, like enterprise software licensing and third-party application development trends
- Open-source adoption trends across small, medium, and large businesses, especially with reference to how OSS is replacing proprietary software
- The adoption of the software-as-a-service (SaaS) and measure the impact on speed, agility, and cost of all of the on-demand/pay-by-the-drink software delivery models
- The location of software applications: how many reside on desktops, laptops, tablets, smartphones, in the cloud? What are the trends?

Devices/People/Tasks Alignment

The adoption of smartphones is outpacing the adoption of just about every technology in history. As form factors have improved, so has functionality. Lots of assumptions have been challenged along the way. For example, how many of us believed that anyone would watch videos on a two-inch by two-inch screen? As it turns out, lots of Gen Xers and Ys, and especially Gen Zs (Zippies), are quite comfortable watching short and long videos on tiny screens. Many of the digerati also believed that soft keyboards would never be accepted by hardcore text messengers. Device adoption is not driven by form factors or exotic functionality, but by connectivity and reliability around basic services. Put another way, the assumptions that the traditional human factors crowd have made over the years about usability, form factors, ease of use, and even aesthetics have not proved valid.

In the 1980s and 1990s we assumed that there should be one corporate machine—the "standard"—blessed by the company's governance policy. We assumed this for several reasons. First, we correctly believed that buying and supporting one machine was cheaper than buying and supporting whatever people felt they needed to do their jobs.

Second, the industry really did not offer us much choice: while there were lots of different PC manufacturers in those days, there were not too many alternative architectures to the venerable Wintel (Microsoft Windows operating systems + Intel chips) machine. Finally, even if the industry gave us a lot of different machines, they would not have been able to communicate with each other. So we were pretty much stuck with the one machine/one employee/one company model. When interoperability standards emerged, everything changed, and when consumerization became a driver of technology adoption, things really changed, and quickly. Now we have all sorts of devices that interconnect. But more to the point, we have multiple devices that satisfy personal and professional computing and communications requirements for a growing percentage of people (employees, customers, suppliers, and partners).

Access devices in 2017 will look, feel, and act differently from one another. Variation will be widely accepted and even encouraged because the relationship between variation and support costs will diminish. *The desirability of machine standardization will yield to the imperative of interoperability standardization.*

Requirements will be defined and discovered around roles and requirements and the devices needed to satisfy those requirements. The distinction between consumer and corporate devices will blur. It just will not matter what devices we use to connect to the Web, our internal databases, and applications, and anything else we need to access in our private or public clouds. Synchronization among devices will be automatic and continuous. Devices will be customizable.

Companies are unlikely to buy PCs or other expensive devices for their employees. *Bring your device to work and we will connect it* is the new mantra by 2017, certainly by 2020. Companies will wean their employees off of their hardware budgets and either provide them an annual credit for their work device or just remove the "benefit" altogether.

There is no question that most of us will access Web content and transaction capabilities via a very thin, throw-away client. We should focus much more on the virtual server than on the device used to access it. In fact, given communications technologies and trends, it makes sense to invest in the "host" much more than the "client." (There is also the digital divide issue: the cheaper the access device, the more people can participate in the ongoing digital revolution.)

Network access in 2017 and forever after will be ubiquitous: we will use desktops, laptops, tablets, smartphones, other thin clients, and a host of multifunctional converged devices to access local area networks, wide area networks, virtual private networks, the Internet, hosted applications on these networks, as well as applications that run locally on (some of) the devices. The networks work pretty well today; tomorrow they will be bulletproof. (The whole Internet of things [IOT]/Internet of everything [IOE] movement will drive this connectivity.)

When the cost falls below $100, companies may provide thin clients to their employees. "Support" equals a basket in the corner of the room. But if thin clients are not deployed, then all bets are off: some—*few, if any, over time*—companies will provide PCs, but most will not and may offer an annual technology credit. As suggested, by around 2017 less than half of the largest enterprises will still be providing free computers with support to their employees. The other half will have moved to providing low-cost thin clients (smartphones, tablets, etc.) or offer a small technology credit.

The big question here is about the form, ownership, and support of the devices we will use to connect to the Web. They will be thin and cheap—we know that—but what about the structure of the device world? Here are some questions:

- What does segmentation look like? Who are the "users" and what do they do? Once we know who and what, we can determine what device is needed.
- Will thin clients (tablets, smartphones, hybrids, etc.) replace desktops, laptops, and other "heavy" devices? Yes, but when and how?
- What will the predominant "thin" architectures look like?
- What do the technology road maps of the device providers look like? Will they provide fully customized access devices?

Analytics Here, Now, and Forever

The push for real-time analytics will drive many data architecture and business intelligence (BI) investments. Real time (RT) is a requirement that will be satisfied by 2017 technology architectures and platforms. RT dovetails with mobility, thin clients, mashups, Web 2.0/3.0, social media, and all of the macro trends that meet on and around 2017.

The torrent of unstructured social media data will overwhelm databases. Open-source platforms like Apache's Hadoop/MapReduce have been designed for large-scale transaction processing of structured and unstructured data. Others are working on social media plug-ins to enterprise customer relationship management (CRM) and enterprise resource planning (ERP) platforms. You get the idea: we are gearing up for collecting and processing massive amounts of unstructured data, which will eventually lead to real-time transaction processing of all kinds.

Structured data will also overwhelm our processing architectures and platforms. Just imagine how much real-time transaction, meter, and performance data is generated every day. Now multiply the amount by some factor of 10 to understand the size of the big data problem (nevermind the size of the *real-time* big data problem).

Here are the questions:

- Will the new BI/analytics technology architecture assume the integration of structured and unstructured data?
- Will next-generation BI/analytics functional architectures embed real-time analysis of structured and unstructured data?
- How will data storage architectures accommodate the structured/unstructured data fire hose?
- How will "database management" be defined in 2017 and beyond? How will traditional relational and object-oriented tools morph to automated collection, analysis, and reporting environments?
- What are the components of the technology road maps of the major BI vendors that speak directly to the new predictive agenda? How are the road maps being operationalized?

Respect Social Media

Social media is on fire. Web 3.0 is the next tsunami.

Wikis, blogs, RSS filters, mashups, crowdsourcing, podcasts, and content tagging/sharing all scream collaboration. Just a couple of years ago, companies were deciding how they were going to ban social networks and larger forms of social media. Now the same companies are learning to embrace social networks and social media. What has changed? Everything—and the changes are permanent.

Social media tools and techniques are extended by location-aware applications. For example, sales and marketing have enormous location opportunities. Knowing where customers are enables real-time personalized marketing: when a restaurateur knows that a customer is 50 yards away from his or her establishment, he or she can offer a deal to get the customer to have breakfast, lunch, or dinner at 20% off the regular price. And why not? Similarly, location awareness enables companies to track shopping habits, travel and delivery routes, among countless other activities.

Social media assumes that there is value in connecting people willing to collaborate through their affinity with people, places, products, and brands. Did anyone really think that Twitter would attract as many people as it has? Customer service and new product releases are especially vulnerable to twittering. Companies now need to worry about what is being said about them in social media. There are now any number of companies that help their clients "listen" to what customers, partners, and employees are saying about them in Facebook, Twitter, MySpace, TripAdvisor, Yammer, and countless other social media. Some of these companies listen, but others, like ListenLogic (http://www.listenlogic.com), extract meaning and purpose from social content, which is what companies really want. Put another way, companies need to know not only *what* people are saying about them, but *why* they are saying what they are saying, *and the response implications of the conversations on products, services, and strategies.*

Web 3.0 represents another technological sea change. Wikipedia defines Web 3.0 as the

> [E]volving development of the World Wide Web in which the meaning (semantics) of information and services on the web is defined, making it possible for the web to understand and satisfy the requests of people and machines to use the web content. It derives from World Wide Web Consortium director Sir Tim Berners-Lee's vision of the Web as a universal medium for data, information, and knowledge exchange.

Just as data was king for Web 1.0 and 2.0, context is king for Web 3.0. Smart search, deep problem-solving, intelligent deduction, and other activities will be enabled by Web 3.0 technologies. In fact, when full context surrounds search, transaction processing, and problem solving, it will fuel proactive behavior and huge amounts of automation—the real Holy Grail of the Web platform. Web 3.0 will evolve toward wider and deeper context, and the Web will continue to grow from repository to enabler. By 2017, much of this context will exist but there will still be a lot to do. There is no question, however, that the ultimate capabilities of the Web will have been outlined and partially experienced by 2017. (By 2020, this whole discussion will seem silly.)

The major research question is about embedded understanding, intelligence, and automation. We need a compass here to keep us on track toward automated, intelligent supply chains, innovation and sales, among other functions. Will it work? What will it cost?

Let us propose a tracking agenda:

- Will social media achieve equal status with structured customer, brand, and related data?
- Will real-time social media become a mandatory corporate requirement?
- Will Web 3.0 arrive on schedule around 2017, or will it be delayed due to chronic limitations of artificial intelligence (AI)?

Innovation, Innovation, and More Innovation

Innovation is everyone's job. Regardless of where anyone sits in an organization, innovation is essential to survival and therefore a core competency of every competitive organization on the planet. But how will 21st century companies innovate?

As a permanent core competency, innovation will be aggressively funded. But significant amounts of funding will not go to internal research and development (R&D) teams, but to teams distributed across the globe through next-generation crowdsourcing. Once the intellectual property (IP) lawyers figure out what to do with advanced crowdsourcing, even conservative companies will rethink their innovation strategies to include crowdsourcing and other Web 2.0/Web 3.0/

ready innovation strategies. Internal crowdsourcing, private cloud crowdsourcing, and open public crowdsourcing will all be viable crowdsourcing options.

Beyond crowdsourcing, by 2017 companies will have multidimensional innovation strategies. They will build open innovation networks consisting of investments, partnerships, incubation, licensing, business process management (BPM), and incentives. Savvy companies will actively pursue seed and early stage investments in companies that can provide innovative solutions. Mergers and acquisitions (M&As) are another piece of the innovation strategy, as are investments in incubators that are ideally located away from corporate headquarters. Licensing is yet another part of the strategy as are investments in BPM, because the reengineering and automation of key business processes is a key innovation methodology. Finally, smart companies understand the power of positive incentives that should be spread throughout and beyond the organization.

BPM will become institutionalized, and software-based collaborative technologies will be merged with hardware-based technologies, especially two-way active radio frequency identification (RFID), adaptive displays, speech recognition, biometric payment systems, and intelligent sensor networks. Sensor technology will emerge as a platform unto itself that enables countless analyses, inferences, and real-time transaction processing. Sensor networks will collect, interpret, and communicate and amplify the capabilities of Web 2.0 and 3.0 technologies, and real-time automation is the end state.

The new technology road map needs depth:

- What are the major software-based innovative initiatives that will drive real-time, automated processing?
- Which hardware-based technologies will augment and amplify which innovative software technologies?
- What forms will "open innovation" actually take? How will its effectiveness be measured?

Missions to the Clouds

When did IT become a competency? Furniture is not a competency. Communications is not a competency. Travel is not a competency. Why is IT a core competency? For some—*very few*—companies,

IT is and should remain a core competency, but for most others, IT is way outside the scope of what companies need to survive and prosper.

Once insightful, candid companies end the core competency dance, they will exploit the acquisition/deployment/support alternatives the industry has provided. The path is simple: infrastructure first, followed by applications and ultimately "platforms." Services around these activities are wide and varied. The major technology vendors, like IBM, Oracle, and Microsoft, have embraced XaaS delivery models, while other vendors, like Salesforce.com, have been champions of alternative delivery models for some time. The credibility that large vendors bring to XaaS is huge and validates the delivery models as "acceptable" and "safe" to large enterprises. Companies will assess the impact that cloud sourcing, including all of the alternative XaaS delivery models (SaaS [software], HaaS [hardware], IaaS [infrastructure], PaaS [platform], CaaS [communications], STaaS [storage], and BIaaS [business intelligence]), will have on their performance. They will assess the impact private clouds will have (while expressing concerns about public cloud security). Cloud architectures will be developed that determine which services are best moved to the cloud, which should stay standardized within corporate firewalls, and what a cloud migration strategy should look like.

Here are the tracking questions:

- What is the rate of adoption of cloud delivery today—and going forward?
- What are the obstacles to cloud adoption, rank ordered by concern, cost, and impact?
- When will internal and external auditors embrace the cloud with a set of standards that work for multiple industries, especially highly regulated industries that require validated technology?

Macro Trends

The technology and technology management trends of the past 30 years seeded the different flavors of technology that are ready now, and changes that will persist for decades. In other words, we are about to reach a new steady state, a kind of business technology convergence that takes the business technology relationship to a new level. (CIOs born before 1970 will become roadkill as the seamless trend unfolds.)

By 2020, operational technology requirements have completely merged with business requirements, and vice versa. There is less distinction now between business and technology than there has ever been. We have gone from business technology *alignment* to business technology *convergence* in just a few decades. Much of the heavy lifting that got us here was due to the efforts of hands-on, in-the-trenches CIOs who worked tirelessly, often in their own self-interest, but tirelessly, nonetheless, to raise the importance of technology at their companies. As it turns out, they may have been *too* successful: we now need their services, at least the services that made them famous, less now than we ever did. Conducting due diligence around the best infrastructure purchases is not what it used to be. Spending months deciding which PCs or tablets to buy is no longer considered a good way to spend professional time. Most of the data center consolidation work has been completed. Thanks to Sarbanes-Oxley and other compliance formulae, we largely solved the backup and recovery problem. E-mail? Word processing? Spreadsheets? These are all old problems, long since solved by dutiful CIOs and their minions.

There is less infrastructure work to do these days. The number of PC and tablet manufacturers has fallen to a handful. The decision space around requirements like security, backup, recovery, storage, and even eDiscovery has narrowed considerably over the past five years. Years ago, we would spend a year or two conducting criteria-based analyses of alternative hardware platforms. Today, those decisions are made in 30 days or less. Not so many years ago, we used our own people to design, deploy, and support our computing and communications infrastructure. Today, we look for smart partners to which we can off-load noncore technology requirements. Eventually, everyone will end up in the cloud. Infrastructure will launch first, followed by applications, and eventually the entire computing and communications platform. The CIOs who survive will be responsible for planning their missions to the cloud. Some of them will do this well and some very poorly: not that many CIOs are deeply skilled in both advanced vendor management and cloud computing—arguably the two most important skills of 2017 and beyond.

Unfortunately, most companies are much better at operational technology than strategic technology. This needs to flip. Strategic technology should move to the business units responsible for profit and loss (P&L). The business managers responsible for strategic applications can source them the same way infrastructure managers will source their applications: from the cloud. The linkage between operational and strategic technology will occur at the architectural standards level. So long as the strategic applications are compliant with the overall enterprise/applications/communications/data architecture, they can be acquired and deployed by the lines of business. This means that requirements, business process modeling, reengineering, and performance metrics all move to the business. This frees us from creating business relationship management offices, enterprise project management offices, and all of the activities we supported over the decades to get technology closer to the business. Just put strategic technology in the business.

Another aspect of all this change is globalization, which will force convergence in several important ways. In fact, globalization is the glue that will strengthen convergence and customization. Where we used to think about common global business processes and one-size-fits-all technology platforms to enable them (like single-instance ERP systems), the future will look very different. While many processes will persist no matter where companies operate globally, many other processes will regionalize and localize. Hub-and-spoke application models will emerge as the flexible alternative to single-instance ERP platforms. This means that functionality will simultaneously globalize, regionalize, and localize based on specific transaction-processing requirements. Multinational corporations will abandon global standardization in favor of decentralized models that emphasize agility and flexibility. While everyone thinks about all of the offices that will be opened as their companies expand, technologists need to also think about all of the offices that will close when things do not go so well. Hub-and-spoke, regional and local, and cloud-based technology delivery models will push global standardization right off the docket.

Is this the end of "IT?" Yes, IT is finally over. It is 2020 and everyone is a CIO, or, more accurately, everyone is a chief business intelligence officer (with advanced degrees in innovation and cloud computing).

While your infrastructure hums in the cloud, all eyes are on ready strategic technology and the businesses now directly responsible and accountable for business technology optimization.

The business technology "alignment" journey will end around 2017. While it may not occur precisely on January 1, 2017, or even in 2018, it will happen. All of the stars are aligned to yield *convergence*. We struggled for decades to get business professionals to talk to technology professionals, to get requirements "right," to define workable governance and organizational structures, and craft budgets that made sense to competing professionals. We also fought a whole lot about unproductive things, like whether HP laptops were better than Dell laptops, if process engineering should precede technology investments, and if business analysts should sit alongside their business partners.

Who should technology report to? First, it was the COO, then it was the CFO, then it was the CEO, then back to the CFO, and then back to the COO—governance, governance, and more (or less) governance. The last quarter of the entire 20th century was devoted to finding the organizational needle in the haystack: the perfect governance structure, which gave us imperfect technology standardization and less-than-perfect though often implemented exception management worst practices. All of this will disappear in the early 21st century.

3
READY PROCESSES

The majority of mature information technology (IT) organizations are organized around sets of overarching technology acquisition, deployment, and support processes. Some focus on people/processes/technology. Some focus on plan/build/run. Others focus on elaborate requirements modeling and demand management. At the end of each process are total cost of ownership (TCO) and return on investment (ROI) calculations.

The processes are deliberate and careful. The industry has told us over and over again that the probability of completing a successful technology project is low. The accepted reasons for this track record are now legendary, including poor requirements analysis, project "scope creep," poor project management, and uncommitted senior management support, among other reasons too numerous to mention here. Many chief information officers (CIOs) and chief technology officers (CTOs) are especially cautious, and thoroughly vet any and all technologies before committing to enterprise implementation.

These processes, and the fear that defines them, need to adapt to ready technology and the premise that ready technologies can dramatically and immediately impact business models and processes. Ready technology requires processes designed to continuously and quickly see/deploy/assess ready technologies. It also requires organizations to work horizontally, because ready technologies can impact corporate functions, processes, strategies, and ultimately, effectiveness.

The essence of ready organization, processes, and governance is the formalization of ready technology assessment and exploitation. There are devices, hardware, and software technologies that 10 years ago were treated as immature and even dangerous, but today and going forward should be identified and vetted as "ready" for implementation. The "rules" around all this are important, especially because they (re-)define a company's technology culture. For many companies this

37

all represents a huge change in the way they see technology, in the way they acquire/deploy/support technology, and in how they define agility (if they define agility at all). Learning how to almost instantly and seamlessly identify, pilot, and deploy ready technologies is a skill that must be developed.

Some companies will find the skills relatively easy to develop or acquire, but others will struggle to change their approach to business technology acquisition, deployment, and support. Companies that have "deliberate" technology acquisition/deployment/support processes will struggle the most: this is not the time for rigid governance models designed to prevent technology investments.

Ready Organization

Figure 3.1 presents enterprise and business unit perspectives on how and where ready technology assessments should occur. Note the usual activities that define most technology organizations. Note also the difference, in federated organizations, between enterprise and business unit IT.

Figure 3.1 suggests that ready technology assessments and formal due diligence should serve both the enterprise and the business units. Note also that the technologies should be assessed with an equally pernicious assessment of business requirements. *In fact, these "requirements TBD" should be reassessed with reference to ready technologies and not just the mature technologies we tend to correlate with well-understood business requirements.* In other words, because many "old" requirements might be satisfied with ready technologies, they should be revisited.

The teams that comprise these new organizations should take the following steps:

- Organize for Ready Technology
- Track Technology Trends
- Vet Promising Ready Technologies
- Pilot the Most Promising Technologies
- Deploy the Ready Technologies across the Enterprise and Business Units
- Continuously Repeat the Steps

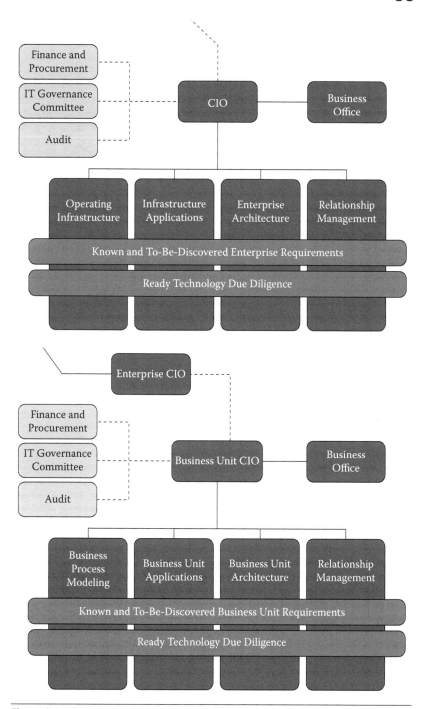

Figure 3.1   Centralized and federated ready technology organizations.

The steps first require ready teams to organize to optimize the ready technology opportunity. They then require companies to formally track technology trends. This requires the ongoing tracking of the research and development (R&D) budgets of technology vendors, where the venture capital industry is placing its bets, and how *Wall Street* defines forward value. It also requires relationships with all of the technology research organizations, pundits, and bloggers. It assumes many conversations and even more traveling. It assumes personnel, budgets for research, consultants and travel, and prestige.

The last assumption—*prestige*—is important: the smartest people at the company should want to be members of the Ready Team. If the best and brightest avoid the Ready mission, it will fail.

Ready Diligence

Ready teams must vet ready technologies. A set of criteria should be used to determine a technology's potential. Here are 10 criteria for vetting ready technologies:

- Is the technology on the right technology/market trends trajectory?
- Is the technology an R&D target for the largest technology vendors?
- Is the technology a target for the private equity venture community?
- Is the technology driving Wall Street valuation models?
- Does the technology have a minimal infrastructure require-ments story?
- Is the technology cost-effective (TCO)?
- Is the technology quantitatively impactful (ROI)?
- Does the technology have a clear differentiation story?
- Can the technology be delivered via the cloud?
- Are competitors vetting the technology?

These criteria are representative of the kinds of criteria clusters that companies can use to vet all varieties of ready technologies.

The methodology should be as structured as possible, as suggested in Figure 3.2. The technologies that score the highest should be immedi-ately piloted, and those that pilot well should be immediately deployed.

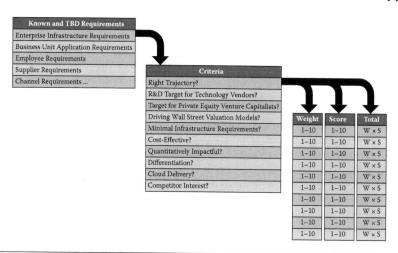

	Known and TBD Requirements			
Enterprise Infrastructure Requirements				
Business Unit Application Requirements				
Employee Requirements				
Supplier Requirements				
Channel Requirements ...				

Criteria	Weight	Score	Total
Right Trajectory?			
R&D Target for Technology Vendors?			
Target for Private Equity Venture Capitalists?			
Driving Wall Street Valuation Models?	1–10	1–10	W × S
Minimal Infrastructure Requirements?	1–10	1–10	W × S
Cost-Effective?	1–10	1–10	W × S
Quantitatively Impactful?	1–10	1–10	W × S
Differentiation?	1–10	1–10	W × S
Cloud Delivery?	1–10	1–10	W × S
Competitor Interest?	1–10	1–10	W × S
	1–10	1–10	W × S
	1–10	1–10	W × S
	1–10	1–10	W × S

Figure 3.2   Ready technology assessment methodology.

Ready Governance

The *governance* around all this is critical. Technology governance—like all corporate governance—is about decision/input rights that describe who is allowed to acquire, deploy, and support business technology. In fully centralized technology organizations, all of the decision rights belong to the centralized control group; in decentralized organizations, decision rights are diffuse; and in federated technology organizations, rights are shared. Companies must decide what works for their industry, leadership, and corporate culture. But without clear, consistent technology governance, companies will, at great risk, underinvest or overinvest in digital technology. They will also inevitably miss important opportunities with ready technologies.

If companies fail to define and implement the right technology governance models, they will be unable to discover or exploit ready technology, unable to adapt quickly to national and global challenges and, perhaps most importantly, unable to quickly evolve ready technology-enabled business models and processes.

Even though ready technologies are all around us, unless there is a plan to optimize their acquisition, deployment, and support, they will barely impact corporate strategies or tactics. Technology governance is the enabler. Technology governance clarifies what should be purchased, how technologies should be deployed, and who should manage—"*own*"—the technology acquisition, deployment, and support process.

The empowerment aspect of governance is what unleashes technology's contribution to growth and profitability. If managers and executives can make the right ready technology investments at the right time, without the constraint of rigid governance structures and processes, technology's contribution to the business can be significant.

Figure 3.3 suggests what governance should look like in a federated organization. Note that Ready Technology is co-owned by the enterprise and business units. This is consistent with the horizontal power of ready technologies (see Figure 3.3).

The governance of ready, and all technology, is critical to the successful piloting and deployment of technology. We are beyond centralized technology acquisition/deployment/support, well beyond 20th century technology governance. Federated governance, especially in the era of ready technology, is the only way to exploit ready technology opportunities.

The key to the exploitation of ready technology is organizational and requirements flexibility. The old sequential technology acquisition/deployment/support processes will never survive the pace of technology change and the volatility of global competition. Companies need to be able to move as quickly as possible to pilot/deploy ready/evolving technologies that will keep them competitive.

Figure 3.3 provides a simple governance matrix, but as we proceed through the 21st century, technology governance is expanding. Figure 3.4 provides a matrix of technologies and participants. It fills each cell in the matrix with a responsible/accountable/consultative/informed (RACI) assignment. RACI charts are popular ways to describe roles. In this case, the roles refer to operational, strategic, and ready technology. But the significance of Figure 3.4 is the sheer size of the matrix and the number of technologies and participants

Actors \ Areas	Enterprise Architecture	Operating Infrastructure	Business Applications	Ready Technology
Enterprise CIO	Decision Rights	Decision Rights	Input Rights	Decision and Input Rights
Business Unit CIOs	Input Rights	Input Rights	Decision Rights	Decision and Input Rights

Figure 3.3 Technology governance.

Technologies / Participants		Operational Technology	Strategic Technology	Ready Technology
Internal	The Enterprise	R/A/C/I	R/A/C/I	R/A/C/I
	Corporate Functions	R/A/C/I	R/A/C/I	R/A/C/I
	Business Units	R/A/C/I	R/A/C/I	R/A/C/I
External	Hardware, Software, and Service Providers	R/A/C/I	R/A/C/I	R/A/C/I
	Partners and Suppliers	R/A/C/I	R/A/C/I	R/A/C/I
	The Crowd	R/A/C/I	R/A/C/I	R/A/C/I

Figure 3.4   Twenty-first century technology governance.

that define where we are and are likely to be for the foreseeable future. Technology deployment, regardless of the class of technology, is no longer controlled by one or two decision makers. In the 20th century, internal decision makers dominated the RACI chart. But as we moved into the 21st century, external decision makers became part of the governance team.

Technology governance is expanding because technology dependency is growing. Companies rely upon cloud providers, social media listeners, and a host of external technologies to operate and grow. Without the participation of hardware, software and service providers, business partners and suppliers, and even the crowd, companies cannot optimize operational, strategic, or ready technology. The playing field has expanded. We now need the external participants as much as we need the internal ones. This is a profound—and permanent—change in the governance of digital technology.

4
READY COMPANIES

Whenever we talk about corporate culture, everyone leans in. Part of the reason for the obsession with corporate culture is that it is personal: everyone feels as though they exhibit the qualities of their corporations and, even more strangely, that corporations have consistent values about anything. Corporate culture is situational and evolving. Changes to the culture can be abrupt when revenue plummets, or gradual when profits remains consistent, or confused when horrible things are said about the company on social media. Of course there are some persistent behaviors and modus operandi, but events, especially big external ones, have a way of changing behaviors (and often leadership teams).

The relevant culture here is a company's technology culture. As I described, companies like Cigna—at least during my tenure—never embraced technology as a corporate weapon. By no means was technology strategic at Cigna. What about your company? Is technology purely operational or optimistically strategic?

Industry cultures define a lot about how companies in different industries acquire, deploy, and support technology. The insurance industry, for example, is a late adopter of technology. If the truth be told, most insurance executives really do not like technology very much. They see technology as a giant annoyance, something they cannot get along without (though wish they could), and something that costs way, way too much money. The major insurance players were all late to the Internet, leaving lots of insurance sales to Internet broker companies like the aforementioned eHealth (http://www.ehealthinsurance.com), not to mention all of the "quote companies" that take money from the insurance companies every time they channel a policy on their behalf. They cling to legacy claims processing systems that have long since crossed the cost/benefit line and are reluctant to make investments in business intelligence and service-oriented architectures. They even still wrestle with build-versus-buy decisions, as though operational technology never commoditized and outsourcing was still just an experiment. What do we give as their overall industry grade—*C*.

The casino industry sees technology as a way to mine data to riches, on the backs of gamblers who lose on Monday, but not Tuesday, and who really like to check into casinos from the back door, among other quirks that together "profile" the high rollers (who lose *lots* of money). Their investments in customer relationship management (CRM) are paying off: they are extracting more money from the high losers than ever before. Their overall industry grade is a *B+* for effectiveness.

The financial services industry is committed to technology on all levels. It is safe to say that they are operational and strategically committed to technology as a lever in their efforts to snare customers (or, as they say, "clients") from cradle to grave. Some banks spend lavishly on technology and some only aggressively. Companies like JP Morgan Chase and Vanguard strongly believe in technology and spend huge amounts of money on new financial products, new service offerings, and especially on the retail end of the business. Vanguard's use of the Web is nothing short of game changing. Their overall industry grade is a *B+*.

The retail industry loves technology—especially the big guys. Wal-Mart, FedEx, Amazon, and UPS, among others, all spend a ton on operational and strategic technology. They have pioneered data warehousing, supply chain management, mobile tracking, and a whole host of cost-saving and revenue-generating projects. Thank these companies every time you track your online packages via the Web. Their grade is an *A-*. (They would have gotten an *A* but they have had a lot of hiccups in the radio frequency identification [RFID] space.)

Industry cultures tell us a lot about technology adoption, the way technology is acquired and sourced, and the expectations that managers and executives have about the contribution technology can make to cost management and revenue generation. What grade would your industry get? Do you know? (I am always amazed at how little we know about our direct and indirect competition.) Take a look around outside of your building. See what your vertical industry is doing with technology. Profile it and your company's approach to technology. Give it a grade within the vertical industry and generally. The answer key should have something to do with using technology to manage costs, technology for strategic advantage, flexible sourcing strategies, and the creative use of performance, customer, and supplier data.

What about attitudes toward change? Where does your company sit on the change continuum? All of the talk about "agility" over the past decade has held corporate mirrors in front of companies that often have agile self-images but seldom actually change anything. When was the last time your company assessed the contributions that technology makes to corporate performance? How long has the technology management team been in place?

There is also corporate organization and governance. How participatory is your company? Or do the few politically connected make all the decisions? If you walked in with an iPad three years ago and told the senior management team that the device would change the company, how would they have reacted?

So what makes a company "ready?" As always, it is a combination of things, including attitude, skills, and technology awareness, among other variables, that together define a ready technology agenda.

Ready Characteristics

Things are changing—again. But this time the changes are more profound and definitely more permanent. We are entering a new era of partnership between technology and business. Technology and business are inseparable now, and business models and processes cannot be implemented without operational, strategic, and ready technology. Technologies like Web 2.0/3.0, business intelligence, cloud computing, and social media are changing the business-technology optimization game. Even the way we think about saving money or making money with technology has changed.

What are the characteristics of ready companies? Here are some:

- Ready companies are continuous and extended: they define transactions as continuous and broad reaching to include all interactions with employees, suppliers, partners, and customers. Ready companies do not define themselves around processing or physical boundaries and do not restrict themselves to traditional technology deployed in deliberate ways.

- Ready companies collaborate and innovate with friends, family, and perfect strangers. Collaboration occurs 24/7 with and among employees, suppliers, customers, partners, and perfect strangers. Collaboration includes communication, negotiations, sharing, design, and innovation, among other activities that traditionally occur inside corporate firewalls.
- Ready companies have diagnostic and evolving core competencies. What the company did well, and essentially, five years ago may no longer be "core" to its current or future success. Ready companies redefine core competencies over time.
- Ready companies provision functionality via alternative delivery models. Why buy when you can rent? Not just technology, but all flavors of business processes. X-as-a-service models pervade ready companies. This proactive provisioning is consistent with the core competency analyses that ready companies conduct.
- Ready companies integrate and interoperate proprietary and open-source technology regardless of the source: ready companies are practical consumers of digital technology and do not routinely subscribe to traditional conventions of standardization for its own sake. Technology that solves problems is highly valued; technology that is elegantly architected but not problem focused is not highly valued.

Ready companies also ask the following kinds of questions:

- What are the internal and external processes that are challenging the status quo? Are you accelerating or resisting them? It is time to rethink, reengineer, and implement processes unconstrained by traditional obstacles, and then invest in speed and agility. For example, are you crowdsourcing innovation?
- What is the conventional, and unconventional, competition doing? It is time to track how you make money, how the competition makes money, and how competitors you rarely see could eat your lunch. You need to become the market share–grabbing unseen competition in your industry. Ready technology, by the way, can help a lot.
- What are the technologies that are changing the game for your industry and your company? Find the list of

technologies that can impact your company in the short term and longer term. Develop a technology watch to pilot to implement list. The short ready list should include business process modeling (BPM), Web 2.0/3.0 technologies, social media, business intelligence/analytics, service-oriented architecture (SOA), virtualization, voice-over-IP (VOIP), thin client architecture, open-source hardware and software, cloud computing, X-as-a-service technology delivery models, Web-platform-based applications, mashups, and crowdsourcing, among other technologies that challenge the legacy platforms and applications that still often dominate our computing and communications infrastructures and architectures.

- How is the Web-as-a-platform transforming your business? It is time to move applications, data, and transaction processing to the Web. It is time to rent, not buy, applications, hardware, communications, and storage. It is time to migrate your internal data center to one in the cloud. If skeptical, move first to a private cloud to test the weather. Over time, you can move to the public cloud to complete the implementation of your likely core competency recommendations.
- How is Web 2.0/3.0 technology changing your business? Wikis, blogs, podcasts, folksonomies, crowdsourcing, virtual reality, social networks, and mashups, among other related technologies, should be assessed according to their contributions to training, marketing, branding, customer service, collaboration, and problem solving. Develop a matrix of Web 2.0/3.0 tools and technologies and business objectives. Implement pilots to test the hypotheses represented in the cells in the matrix. For example, could wikis replace your training content and learning management system?
- How is social media changing your company and your business? Accept that, like the telephone, the mix of personal versus professional activity cannot be policed. Start listening to your employees, suppliers, and customers. Stop hoarding information and start sharing it. Invest in internal and external collaboration. Crowdsource as many activities and processes as is legally and strategically possible.

- Is technology required to save you money, make you money, improve your services, and/or help you comply? What is the priority? Figure out information technology (IT)—and fast. Does your company want IT to deliver more cost savings than revenue generation? Is IT focused on compliance? Improving services? Make sure your investments align with your priorities.

- Are you rethinking your core competencies regarding technology? Is IT still high on the list? This is a continuous process. Ready is about agility, efficiency, extensibility, collaboration, and continuity. Is IT part of that equation? Now it is time to identify what you do well, poorly, and not at all but should absolutely be doing better. While corporate identities are always tough to define, it is essential to know who you are—and who you are not—going forward.

- Are alternative technology delivery models under serious consideration? Is cloud computing high on the list, or is there still considerable skepticism about outsourcing? Have you entered the cloud through software-as-a-service, hardware-as-a-service, communications-as-a-service, or some other X-as-a-service delivery model? Now it is time to pilot X-as-a-service delivery models. It is time to develop a plan to test as many alternative delivery models as possible. Develop vendor partnerships that will reduce the time, effort, and cost of diagnostic pilots. Develop a "fail fast/fail cheap" piloting strategy. IT is ready.

- When was the last time you conducted a business technology optimization audit? This is another continuous process. It is important to benchmark your performance on all levels. What are you doing well and what are you doing poorly, and expensively? You need an audit template that you exercise on a scheduled basis. At the very least, the audit should focus on people, processes, and technology. Include your use of ready technology in the next audit.

- Do you have a set of save money/make money/improve services/compliance quantitative performance metrics that measure the business value of technology? Metrics should be quantitative, transparent, and publicized. The list should be vetted by all business and technology stakeholders.

- How are you governed today? How should you be governed tomorrow? How are decision and input rights distributed at your company? How should they be distributed? Now is the time to identify, define, and distribute the decision and input rights around IT principles, architecture, infrastructure, applications, and investment processes. The process should be collaborative and aligned with the corporate culture and the preferences of the senior management team. Note that things have changed: does enterprise IT really need to "control" everything? Probably not. Seek the right balance of control, authority, and accountability across the enterprise and the business units.

- How should you organize for ready? How should you organize globally? How centralized/decentralized should you be? Do you still need an "office of the chief information officer (CIO)?" Do you need a program management office (PMO), a vendor management office (VMO), and a business technology management office (BTMO)? What other offices do you need? It is time for a VMO—how can you enter the cloud without acquisition/deployment/support expertise? It is time to invest in expertise around sourcing, request for proposal (RFP) development, service-level agreements (SLAs), and performance management. It is the same for your PMO. It is also time for a new BTMO office to manage the demand/supply issues around technology investments. As the need for more technology rises, there is a growing need to transparently coordinate supply and demand and proactively manage expectations through results. Accountability and reporting relationships should also be reengineered. Against your governance framework, what control should be federated and what should be closely held?

- Do you have ready people? Are they smart enough? Dedicated enough? Incentivized enough? Agile enough? When was the last time you conducted a skills/competencies gap analysis? What is the plan for filling the gaps? If necessary, can you switch out people at your company or are you politically constrained? Chances are you do not have among your staff deep expertise in ready technologies. You need to immediately conduct a skills gap analysis and acquire the skills and competencies you lack. The list is likely to be long. You need to break through the good 'ol boy (and gal) protocols that often define human resources (HR). If you cannot break the old protocols you will undermine your ability to compete and never enable the exploitation of ready technology.

• Do you have the right business technology leadership? This is a tough one but integral to your company's membership in the ready club. The hard and soft skills and competencies necessary to excel in the early 21st century are quite different from those that defined success in the 20th century. The right leadership will get you there; the wrong leadership will keep you anchored in the 20th century. Without casting any dispersion on "older" technology leaders, and certainly not intending to invite any lawsuits regarding age discrimination, it is more likely that a Gen Xer or Yer will relate better to ready technology than Baby Boomers born before 1965.

Ready Context

Politics is one aspect of the overall context that influences decisions. The others include the culture of the company, the quality and character of the leadership, the financial condition of the company, and the overall financial state of the industry and the national and global economies.

This context of politics/culture/leadership/company/economy explains a lot about what and how all technology decisions are made. They are also the "soft" or "intangible" factors that are sometimes overlooked by overzealous technologists who for the life of them just cannot understand why a really great technology idea gets little more than a polite nod. Maybe the answer lies somewhere in the overall context in which business technology decisions are always made.

It is important to assess the political quotient of your company. Some companies are almost completely "political": a few people make decisions based only on what they think, who they like (and dislike), and what is good for them personally (which may or may not be good for the company). Other companies are obsessive-compulsive about data, evidence, and analysis. In the middle are most of the companies out there, with some balance between analysis and politics. Where would you locate your company?

Ready decisions are also made in the context of the financial condition of your company, your industry, and the national and global economies in which you operate. If your company is bleeding revenue, no new investments will be welcomed. Occasionally, a bleeding company may try to stop the bleeding with new investments, but most companies stop spending when revenue starts hemorrhaging.

Fear also results from national and global economic slowdowns. Companies get cautious when they see their long-term prospects threatened. Track all dimensions of the context in which corporate strategies and tactics are implemented.

Ready Risk Management

It may well be that what companies do not do creates the greatest risk. In other words, what about the risk of strategies that minimize risk by making the funding criteria so stringent that hardly any projects make it through the vetting process? What is the risk of a bad strategy? What is the risk of yielding to the inertia of "how we do things?" What is the risk of avoiding ready technologies?

Strategic risk should be measured differently than operational risk. Strategic risk should be forward thinking, proactive, and opportunity driven. In fact, the cost of not doing something should be measured creatively and—as counterintuitive as it may seem—quantitatively.

So what are the strategic opportunities that are simultaneously risks? First, it is the management of the overall business technology relationship. While the debate about "alignment" has persisted for decades, the realities of the agile organization have passed the debate by, and ready dovetails perfectly with agility.

No one needs to argue about the importance of IT any longer. No one needs to think about reporting relationships that will encourage communication among business and technology professionals. We are way past all that. The question now focuses on how wide and deep the relationship should be and the consequences of defining the relationship poorly.

Business technology relationship management (BTRM) is an opportunity and a risk. When done right it can increase the payoff of technology investments. When done poorly or not at all, it can cost a company money, time, and employee productivity. The risk impact of avoiding BTRM is very high. Ready technology opportunities and risks need to be specifically communicated throughout your company.

The next strategic risk is sourcing. Only someone who has lived on another planet for the past few years would be unaware of the impact of alternative technology delivery models. While core competency assessments are something we have all done from time to time, the need for them now is at an all-time high. Competition can be found down the road or across the globe. If a company is making or servicing the wrong things, with the wrong processes and cost structures, they will die from the blow of a competitor who might just as well be invisible as in their face. Such is the result of the eBusiness bandwagon we all so eagerly jumped onto in the late 1990s. Understanding what business works and what does not is paramount to 21st century companies. Is the acquisition, deployment, and support of operational, strategic, and ready technology part of the expertise a company wants or needs to have? Should companies continue to home-grow and customize technology? Or has it become fully commoditized? The strategic risk of getting sourcing wrong is huge. As suggested throughout this discussion, ready technologies rely upon cloud delivery for rapid/low-cost/low-risk deployment.

What about business process modeling and new business models? How can a business remain competitive and efficient without understanding, at a detailed level, the processes that together define its business model? How can a company invest in manual BPM when there are countless software tools that enable even the most complicated modeling? (Yes, there are still many companies who keep their business processes modeled on paper and, maybe, in a spreadsheet.) The risk of not doing BPM is similar to the risk of never going to the doctor or getting a blood test. You do not know what you do not know, which makes many managers happier than knowing about processes they have to improve.

Investments in new technology present opportunities and risks. What is the risk of avoiding ready technologies? Or coming so late to the party that the lights are already off? Here are three examples: virtualization, analytics, and software as a service (SaaS). Virtualization saves money—sometimes lots of money. Analytics makes money.

SaaS relieves all kinds of pressure from already strapped internal technology staffs. A few years ago all of these technologies, while doing fine, were not what most analysts would have called "mainstream." But now they are fully exploitable. While jumping in now makes sense, jumping in a couple of years ago made much better sense. We are not talking about early adoption of bleeding-edge technologies here. We are talking about the monitoring of technologies likely to pay large dividends to those who adopt them at the right time and place in their evolution. The ability to do this is a strategic capability. Existing without this capability is risky and expensive.

What about investments in people? How many corporate strategies talk about the importance of "talent management?" How many actually mean it? Words are easy and cheap. Investments are the indicators of strategic value. At the end of the day, without the right people all organizations suffer. What is the risk of losing your best people? What is the risk of having your best people recruited away? What is the risk of keeping your people well-steeped in old technology? What about ready technology people? Do you have any?

These strategic opportunities/risks will define success. One simple drill is to ask why ready technologies have not been deployed. Assess the response. Is the answer "we do not have enough money to fund things like this?" Is it "these kinds of things only generate soft ROI?" Or, is it "we have tried these kinds of things in the past and they did not work out?" These are the answers of managers and executives willing to accept the risks associated with the failure to make the right strategic decisions. The trick is to develop a list short enough to attract the no-brainer crowd.

Put another way, who can oppose strategic decisions that increase value and reduce risk? Try finding someone willing to say that they do not believe in investing in their people, or that ready technologies are all hype, or that insight into the company's business processes is unnecessary? Ask what the feeling is about improving the relationship between the business and technology professionals at the company. Or how does everyone feel about optimizing the company's relationships with its vendors?

Strategic risk discussions are especially important today because of the nature, location, and speed of competitors. The days of "owning" a market are long gone. Companies struggle on a daily basis to survive, let alone grow profitably. The irony is that when times are tough we focus on the operational and tactical, squeezing as much money from these areas as we can. But the real money lies in strategic initiatives with longer tails. It is a pity that so many managers see crises as green lights to cut costs (and people and processes) rather than launch the right long-term strategic initiatives. Is your company tactically tight but strategically weak? Maybe it is time to reassign the risk police to more important duties.

Ready technology processes will be attacked by the standards police, project terrorists, and anyone else threatened by new ways of thinking about old problems. At the end of the day, this is all about leadership. Some companies have it, and some do not.

Ready IT

Information technology (IT) is changing *again*. In order to understand ready opportunities, it is important to understand the trajectory of IT in many companies today and going forward.

The organization, delivery, and governance of IT has changed before, but this time the changes are permanent. They all clear the way for ready technology pilots and the deployment of ready technology.

There are three major *drivers* of this change:

- Accelerating Consumerization
- Available "Ready" Technologies
- Growing "Participatory Governance"

There will be three major *outcomes* of this change:

- Postfederated/Decentralized Technology Adoption and Delivery
- Agile Technology-Enabled Business Models and Processes
- A Restructured Business Technology Marketplace

The Drivers

Consumerization

Everyone has stories about how personal technology made its way into their companies. The explosion and availability of technology capable of solving countless personal productivity and business problems forever changed the technology adoption process. iPhones and iPads were well in use before IT organizations declared them safe or made them standard issue. The same is true of Skype, Dropbox, Expensify, and Basecamp, among a growing number of technologies and technology-enabled services.

Consumerization is about a technology repertoire enabled by major and nonmajor vendors that sell *or gift* directly to individuals. Consumers adopt these technologies on their own and share them among their friends and colleagues. But the difference today is that consumerized technologies now solve *business* problems, and they do so easily and cost-effectively.

Often to the chagrin of the IT staff, consumerization is now as much a part of technology acquisition and delivery as the due diligence teams that filled countless conference rooms for decades. Instead of endless vendor presentations about just how great their technologies are, consumers now routinely try and buy technologies quickly and cheaply from the consumerized infrastructure and applications marketplace.

These trends are accelerating. More of the technology hard at work inside companies has its roots in a smartphone or tablet. Advertisers, friends, bloggers, and family all keep the lists current: look at the number of times you have heard about a new technology from friends versus the number of times you have heard about technology from your IT department. This process will not change.

Employees (aka consumers) vote their digital preferences with laptops, tablets, smartphones, and applications that make them productive, not from votes cast by their technology managers. They go to the cloud to store documents and data, host digital meetings, and find productive applications. Sometimes these clouds are part of their company's delivery infrastructure, but increasingly they are not. The same employees are also seeking advice in "the crowd" (the consumerized help desk) where opinions, expertise, and problem solving are instantly and continuously available.

Ready Technology

As discussed throughout this book, 20th century technology adoption models were predicated on the diagnosticity of business requirements and technology maturity. The assumption was that technology and business requirements evolve at a pace that justifies phased technology adoption. Early deployments were assumed to be risky, costly, and therefore unnecessary.

As mentioned, defined business requirements were prized. As discussed, an enormous industry was created around "requirements analysis," "requirements modeling," and "requirements validation." Books, articles, conferences, and workshops were everywhere. The prevailing wisdom was that business requirements modeling and validation were prerequisites to technology adoption, and that structured pilot demonstrations with compelling TCO and ROI results were necessary to justify deployment. Technology also had to integrate and interoperate with existing technology infrastructures and architectures. If it failed to cost-effectively integrate, adoption was often halted. If it did integrate, then a structured transition period was defined to test and deploy the new technology before the technology went into "production." Finally, "new" technology, just like old technology, required continuous support and expensive refreshes.

Technology adoption is different today. "Requirements" are often undefined and driven by employees-consumers who adopt technologies to solve a variety of problems with technologies that are acquired, and sometimes even supported, way outside the corporate firewall.

Consumer-driven requirements analysis, exploration, *and discovery* is the mainstay of ready technology adoption. Note also that what we previously described as controlled pilots are today largely ad hoc opportunistic experiments that sometimes quickly turn into technology deployments, with or without the approval of corporate IT. Support is provided by ready technology vendors who also keep the technology current (even as they perform backups).

There are a growing number of technologies ready to go to work immediately. Many of these technologies are cloud based, open source, and live outside corporate firewalls. Many of them are easily and inexpensively accessible to corporate professionals and will therefore continue to find their way into companies of all shapes and sizes, regardless of what CIOs think about the readiness of the technologies.

Participatory Governance

In the 20th century, governance was largely about technology standards and control. As we moved into the 21st century things began to change, first from centralized to federated and then, more recently, to "participatory." Governance now involves more stakeholders than it ever did, most of which live outside the corporate firewall. Participatory governance is emerging as the postfederated governance model.

In fully centralized technology organizations, all of the decision rights belong to an enterprise control group; in decentralized organizations, decision rights are diffuse, spread across the enterprise and the business units; and in federated technology organizations, rights are shared across the enterprise, the business units, and even specific corporate functions.

Since the mid-1990s, the governance pendulum has swung wildly. In the mid- to late-1990s, technology was considered strategic. After the dot.com crash in 2000 the pendulum swung back to operational control. It stayed that way until 2003 when technology budgets began to increase again. The pendulum swung from operational to strategic again where governance was shared between the enterprise CIO and the business unit CIOs (or just the business unit technology directors). We stayed on this course until the world melted down again in 2008 and the governance pendulum swung all the way back to total budget lockdown where governance was centralized in the hands of a few, or just one, senior executives like the chief financial officer (CFO), the chief operating officer (COO), or infrequently, the chief executive officer (CEO).

During all this swinging, something changed. Almost as though it was clandestinely taking advantage of budgetary distractions, technology freed itself from the control of both enterprise and business unit professionals. It escaped from all of the arguments that had it swinging back and forth for decades. In fact, it rendered the "control" word moot: *technology commoditized and consumerized*. It also finalized the near-total dependency business has on the reliability, scalability, reach, and security of its digital technology. Put another much simpler way, business cannot function or exist without information technology (IT)—and everyone knew IT.

In spite of the warnings and trepidations, business units are now aggressively adopting new technologies. Consumerized, cloud-delivered technology has changed the rules around acquisition, deployment, and support. Business units no longer ask corporate IT if they can rent software or buy iPads. They just rent and buy as they choose, often without even telling IT about what they have done.

"Shadow IT" is bigger than ever.* The ability of business units to do what they please is fueled by the technology itself. Cloud computing—renting rather than buying technology—and easily supported devices like smartphones and tablets make it easy for anyone to acquire, deploy, and support digital technology. The new cloud-based technology delivery models and the proliferation of consumerized devices and applications have completely changed the governance game.

The Outcomes

Postfederated/Decentralized Technology Adoption and Delivery

Within five years, IT "departments" will disappear in many companies. "Technology" will merge with business models and processes, or more accurately, become seamlessly immersed in business models and processes. The technology function will exist across the businesses fueling numerous business activities and processes, like sales, marketing, finance, customer service, innovation, and supply chain management, among all of the business functions and activities that comprehensively define a company's business models and processes.

In practice, this means that there will be "technologists" on all of the business teams. It means that there will be sales technologists, marketing technologists, finance technologists, customer service technologists, innovation technologists, and supply chain management technologists, among others who understand both business processes and models and current and emerging digital technology.

---

* "Shadow IT" is what the industry refers to as "unauthorized" technology spending. Many business units buy their own technology without the participation or knowledge of the central/corporate technology organization. Shadow IT can be as high as 2% to 3% of gross revenue, especially in weakly, or inappropriately, governed organizations.

These business technologists will be opportunistic. They will acquire and deploy technology as quickly and cheaply as possible. They will do so because they will be (business unit) *project*, not (enterprise) *standards*, driven. They will be problem solvers working side by side with their colleagues in the business functional areas. Many of them will also work side by side with their customers and suppliers, because digital technology is the glue of business.

Enterprise IT—what we now describe as the keepers of a company's technology infrastructure—will also move. But unlike what we describe today as "business partners," infrastructure jockeys will move to enterprise audit. They will pursue a three-pronged agenda: architecture, infrastructure, and security. Enterprise IT in corporate audit? It is a natural fit. Audit already owns security and operational performance. The addition of the architecture function is consistent with Audit's role as an optimizing group responsible for making things consistent, compliant, and measurable. After it moves to Audit, enterprise IT—responsible for infrastructure activities like e-mail, storage, backup, and recovery—will do what operational IT does best: deliver secure, recoverable basic services as cheaply as possible. The architecture function is important because it will assure that the technology the lines of business deploy will not crash networks or corrupt infrastructure applications. Audit is the best place to enforce the architectural standards that enterprise IT groups have failed to enforce for decades. Audit is also the best place for another new core competency: cloud and applications service-level agreement (SLA) negotiations and management. Since procurement is often part of the larger Audit team anyway, it is a natural place to locate cloud SLA management.

Agile Technology-Enabled Business Models and Processes

Agile is still all the rage—and why not? Anytime anyone can simultaneously attack a slow/expensive/ineffective process and replace it with a better/cheaper/faster one, there is happiness all the way around. Agile is about the role that technology plays in business problem solving. Agile is financially unconstrained. Where we previously invested huge amounts of capital in technology assets that locked us into long-term amortization commitments, today we invest operating dollars in technology assets we have never met and to which we have no long-term financial relationship. The whole technology acquisition and deployment process is now fluid, dynamic, and unconstrained.

Cloud delivery enables agility, while offering low-cost infrastructure and applications. Low-cost (and sometimes free) applications enable agility. Business technology pilots are not designed to validate discrete requirements but to discover new continuous ones. If none are discovered you can then move to the next technology-inspired solution. This is agility.

The conventional approach to technology acquisition and design has been replaced by visits to the app store and the cloud. The number of truly new applications design and development projects has fallen dramatically and will continue to fall. The agile versus systems development life cycle (SDLC) argument is just not that relevant or interesting anymore.

In the context of organizational change, agile refers to the approach that companies take to technology acquisition and delivery. *We can invest and divest in the same day,* which was not conceivable in the 20th century. Invest-and-divest agility impacts every aspect of business. Technology-enabled models and processes are quickly discoverable, modifiable, discardable, and reconstitutable. The more "agile" the company, the more competitive it will be, without the financial drag of old technology acquisition and delivery cycles.

A Restructured Business Technology Marketplace

The technology marketplace is still largely controlled by a relatively small number of vendors. IBM, HP, Microsoft, Cisco, Dell, EMC, Oracle, and a few others own a disproportionate percentage of the corporate technology market.

But this is changing quickly. Some new entrants like Amazon, Rackspace, and Apple are now serving more companies and eating into the market share of the perennial elephants. Perhaps more importantly, the number of *ready technology vendors* is growing dramatically.

The *Wall Street Journal* reports that an increasing number of companies are buying from emerging or even start-up technology vendors (Worthen, 2012). Others report that emerging technologies are becoming mainstream technologies almost overnight (Currier, 2011). This is a huge change and is directly related to the need for speed and agility. In fact, Currier (2011) reports that the drivers of emerging technology adoption include "improving business agility, creating cost savings or productivity enhancements, and opening up new markets or opportunities for the enterprise" (p. 1). Many old-school technology buyers and vendors operate within a waterfall procurement process with distinct steps that eventually lead to procurement. The new technology adoption process is much more about speed and relevance and rapid assessments about the contribution that the technology is (or is not) making to the company.

Companies need speed and agility, and the structure of the new marketplace will continue to satisfy these demands. Established technology vendors must adapt to the new technology delivery models even as they struggle with some profit loss: vendors make more money, for example, from licensing enterprise software to their clients versus clients paying only for what they use. Smaller vendors will attack the markets previously owned by the major established vendors resulting in a much wider set of vendor options for customers seeking fast/cheap/adaptive solutions to their well- *and* ill-defined requirements.

The impact of the new ready technology marketplace will be profound. It will expand the horizons of the enterprise and business units. It will legitimize the inclusion of vendors, products, and services that 10 years ago would never have been piloted. The new marketplace will also empower ready technology vendors who used to think that they had no chance of landing a large account in an IBM or HP shop. But the real impact of the new marketplace will be increased innovation and creativity.

Figure 4.1 suggests what the new structure will look like. Note that much of what we today describe as operational technology is now reporting to enterprise audit and the CFO (to which Audit usually reports). Operational technology consists of desktops, laptops, tablets, smartphones, servers, and the policies and procedures for acquiring, supporting, and securing them. Audit also owns architecture and the principles by which technology integrates and interoperates. The business units own their (marketing, finance, sales, manufacturing, supply chain, quality control, etc.) processes and the digital applications that support all of these processes. They also own business technology innovation.

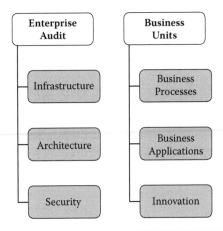

Figure 4.1   The reorganization of IT.

Enterprise audit and the business units will acquire and deliver technology via the cloud, app stores, and other consumerized venues. IT as we know it today will vanish like a disassembled old car sold off for parts. But the parts will reassemble in ways that will enable the exploitation of ready technology delivery models and business agility. The drivers of this change are all around us and unlikely to abate.

What about the technology professionals who will populate this new world? Many of them will fully immerse themselves into the business units. Others will end up in Audit. The skills and competencies going forward will not change as much as where they are applied. While there will definitely be some new skills and competencies, such as cloud SLA design and management, many of the full-immersion skills and competencies already exist in our best business relationship managers. The best infrastructure jockeys know how to optimize basic services, regardless of where they sit.

Budgeting will follow the lead that the federation has already defined. Enterprise budgets for infrastructure, architecture, and security will be raised by taxing the business units, who will self-fund their own technology investments, including investments in ready technology.

This brave new technology world will be quite different from the one with which most of us are familiar. Depending on your perspective, the changes may be revolutionary or evolutionary.

5
READY INDUSTRY PILOTS

How will ready technologies impact various industries?

What ready technology pilots should they launch to exploit what the technologies can do?

Let us look at three industries:

- Higher Education
- Retail
- Healthcare

Higher Education

We begin with the higher education industry.

It is no secret that the cost of higher education is increasing way too rapidly: students routinely go into huge debt to earn their undergraduate and graduate degrees. It is also no secret that the "pedagogy" around the delivery of courses and curricula has not changed much in decades— some would say even centuries. There is also learning. Are we sure that students learn as well as they can with the current "delivery" model?

How might ready technologies help?

Use the technology clusters discussed in Chapter 1 and throughout the book:

- Cloud
- Architecture
- Social Media
- Big Data Analytics
- Bring Your Own Device (BYOD)
- Interfaces
- Thin and Wearable Devices
- Internet of Things (IOT)/Internet of Everything (IOE)
- Location-Based Services
- Automation

How can higher education exploit these ready technologies?

As already suggested, one of the major strengths of *cloud computing* is the freedom it provides companies—*and colleges and universities*—to think operationally and strategically about how they want to leverage digital technology. Instead of worrying about network latency and server maintenance, technology professionals in higher education can focus on innovation, sales, and marketing, among other activities (within and beyond the cloud). Another strength is flexibility. Picking from a menu is easier than designing one, and then delivering the food. Scalability is often just a phone call, e-mail, or alert away. The freedom from software maintenance, denial-of-service attacks, software version control, viruses, backup, and recovery, and other academic operational headaches is provided by cloud computing (assuming the cloud provider is competent, of course).

Higher education can exploit all kinds of cloud services. First, colleges and universities can move massive amounts of operational and strategic technology to the ready cloud. There is no reason for universities to run their own computing and communications power plants. In fact, just about everything a college or university does today can occur in the cloud. But perhaps most importantly, colleges and universities can immediately pilot cloud-based learning management systems (LMSs) like Blackboard, which they may already be hosting on their campuses. They can also immediately pilot the use of massively open online courses (MOOCs), which can be used to deliver courses far and wide with a small investment in delivery infrastructure. While the MOOC "freemium" model may not work for all colleges and universities, it should be immediately piloted.

Colleges and universities can also pilot cloud-based course and curricula development models where faculty design and store their course content, cases, and overall pedagogy. Demonstrating how ready technology can impact processes and standardization, colleges and universities might require faculty to use specific cloud-based services.

Ubiquitous cloud delivery can permeate the entire university community—all students, faculty, and administrators. The pilot might consist of a suite of cloud providers, some of which would be "safer" than others. The pilot might measure the effectiveness, reliability, and security of alternative cloud providers, among other performance metrics.

Distributed architectures, application programming interfaces (APIs), and software components are yielding rapid-active versus slow-passive software design. Instead of rigid, embedded processes, active software architectures enable the addition or subtraction of functionality through component architectures and APIs that will grow increasingly flexible and be available from a variety of sources including the original authors of the software and all kinds of software mercenaries. Open-source APIs will make it possible to reengineer functional designs in near real time. Software will be designed in interoperable pieces, not monolithic structures. APIs and other components will enable functional interoperability, extensibility, and adaptability. The integration of disparate cloud delivery technologies is also part of the trend toward architecture compatibility, which is extremely important to the adoption of ready technology.

All of this can be exploited in higher education. Open architectures are the hallmark of many university infrastructures. Open-source APIs can be used by the universities or by their providers. Integration and interoperability are realistic goals: colleges and universities should pilot as many APIs as possible.

App stores represent a whole new software development and distribution channel, and higher education can continuously avail itself of these apps. The cost of piloting new apps is minimal. Some of these apps can support the educational mission and some the administrative mission, but most of them are mobile, so they support the whole mission without anchors to time, places, or hosts.

As discussed, social media is everywhere. *Social business intelligence* is the goal for companies, colleges, and universities. The intersection of traditional structured data (about students and competitors) and unstructured social data (from Facebook, Twitter, YouTube, forums, and blogs) represents opportunities for next-generation business intelligence and predictive analytics. The billions of posts, tweets, and blogs every month represent the richest communications and collaboration channel in history. Ready colleges and universities are developing formal and permanent social media listening and analysis strategies as we speak. It is important to explore the options and weigh the results against a set of listening/analysis/engagement goals (which, ideally, are derived from an explicit higher education social media strategy).

At Villanova University, Villanova, Pennsylvania, we listen to students, parents, and competitors. We want to understand what everyone and anyone says and thinks about Villanova. We want to understand what students and parents say and think about Boston College, Notre Dame, Georgetown, and Wake Forest, our competitors. We need to understand student motivations and their fears. We need to know what they like and dislike, and we need to know this continuously and ideally in real time. We have piloted several social media listening platforms. All of them are hosted externally: we provide our listening and intelligence requirements and the vendors fire up their technologies. *These pilots have been inexpensive and immediate—the essence of ideal ready technology pilots.* Changing vendors presents no special problems. Changing the listening/analysis parameters presents no problems: we can easily change when/where/how we listen/analyze with an e-mail (or text message, or even a tweet).

Higher education should avail itself of ready social media technology to enable the following:

- Higher Education Market Research
- Specific College/University Brand Management
- Competitive Intelligence
- Educational Product/Service Innovation and Life Cycle Management
- Student/Faculty Services

The *real-time big data analytics* challenge is real and growing. "Data" are no longer owned by the enterprise. They are created by everyone: students, faculty, partners, managers, strangers, bloggers, and vagabonds, among anyone else who would like to offer insights, solve problems, or buy educational products and services.

The end game is simple: real-time descriptive, explanatory, predictive, and prescriptive data, information, and knowledge about internal and external processes and performance. But there are challenges. The amount of data streaming into colleges and universities today is huge and growing.

The power of analytics is clear: the more descriptive, explanatory, predictive, and prescriptive insight a college or university has, the better its operational and strategic performance. The ability to observe and tune operations and strategy, especially in real time, is essential to competitive positioning and growth. Analytics is awareness and engagement. Colleges and universities that ignore analytics will weaken their ability to compete and improve.

Big data analytics pilots in higher education should focus on a variety of descriptive, explanatory, and predictive outcomes. Here are some simple questions that should focus analytics in higher education:

- What degrees will be in the highest demand in the next five years? Ten years?
- What are the current demographics of the college/university and the demographics of the major competitors? What will they be in five years? Ten years?
- How many professors will retire over the next five years? Ten years?
- What will tuition be in five years? Ten years?

Most of these are strategic questions that demand timely answers. The technologies that generate the answers include standard database management systems (DBMSs) and tools designed specifically for structured and unstructured big data analytics, such as Hadoop, which should be installed and used to ask and answer the above kinds of questions. Hadoop is far from perfect, but it is ready.*

BYOD is already at work, even at colleges and universities. We are all familiar with the model. Employees, suppliers, and partners are encouraged to use whatever digital devices they prefer while working in, or interacting with, your company (or college/university). Some believe that the BYOD movement is about reducing corporate technology expenses, while others believe that happy employees/suppliers/partners are productive employees/suppliers/partners. It is a fast-moving trend that is uncovering many issues that companies and their technology providers are quickly addressing.

---

* "Apache™ Hadoop® is an open-source software project that enables the distributed processing of large data sets across clusters of commodity servers. It is designed to scale up from a single server to thousands of machines, with a very high degree of fault tolerance. Rather than relying on high-end hardware, the resiliency of these clusters comes from the software's ability to detect and handle failures at the application layer." See http://hadoop.apache.org/. Also see Gary Nakamura, "Why Hadoop Only Solves a Third of the Growing Pains for Big Data," *Wired Magazine*, January 24, 2014 (http://www.wired.com/insights/2014/01/hadoop-solves-third-growing-pains-big-data/).

Colleges and universities wrestle with BYOD all the time. Some colleges and universities actually provide free computers to their incoming students. Villanova University has provided laptops to our incoming freshmen and women for years. We even provide new ones after two years that the students are allowed to keep after graduation. But the model is weakening. Many incoming students already, obviously, have their own machines. The ready technology pilots here include first a modified process that stops the allocation of laptops to incoming students. The next one looks at devices altogether differently. *What's ready today? Tablets with educational applications. Wearables with location awareness.* We have begun a pilot to explore the use of Google Glass and iPads. The iPads will possibly be handed out to incoming students (instead of laptops). They will be preloaded with courses, course content, eLearning platforms, and supporting learning applications. Online/offline/blended learning will be tested. In the spirit of BYOD, students with their own tablets will also participate in the new learning pilot. In fact, since the educational architecture will not be anchored to a specific hardware platform, all devices will be compatible with the preloading, cloud-delivered pilot. This enables BYOD while preserving one of the ways that Villanova differentiates itself from the competition—free devices for students and faculty.

The Google Glass pilot is in the hands of students who will determine how Glass can be used to learn and communicate. Villanova selected some students to pilot Glass and the applications that extend its functionality. We are looking at Glass as well as additional "wearables" to determine how they might enhance the educational experience. The pilot will determine how we use Glass for educational purposes.

The *interfaces* we use to interact with hardware and software of all kinds are changing. Speech input is becoming more capable, and other interface technology like gesture control is also gaining momentum. Displays are becoming more interactive and intuitive: "visualization" was impressive in the 1990s, and today it is essential and intelligent. Biometrics are now, after many years, moving mainstream. While there were deployments of biometric technology in selected industries and for specific purposes, the iPhone has finally consumerized biometric authentication. Facial recognition technology (and other biometric interfaces) is also advancing at a rapid pace. Such technology will facilitate access to, and other "controls" of, devices, processes, and transactions.

Since writing is such a huge part of teaching and learning experiences, higher education should pilot all varieties of speech input. Speech applications should be preloaded onto the architecture that supports faculty and students, both prodigious writers and communicators. In fact, voice recognition technology has been ready for some time. It is surprising that adoption has been so slow. As discussed, many companies, colleges, and universities often do not like change of any kind. Perhaps this explains why (really) ready voice recognition technology is not widely adopted in higher education.

The same is true of biometrics, which can be easily and quickly piloted. As more security breaches occur, and as the impact of the breaches increases, biometric authentication is ready, willing, and able to address a wide variety of security challenges. Higher education is a fishbowl in constant need of protection.

Thin and wearable is definitely here. Most of us access the Internet with a *"thin" device*. Increasingly, these devices are *on* or even *in* us. While we still use desktops and laptops, increasingly we use tablets, smartphones, and other thin clients to access local area networks, wide area networks, virtual private networks, the Internet, hosted applications on these networks, as well as applications that run locally on (some of) the devices. The economics are so compelling for thin clients that we can expect the "fat" corporate PC and the venerable laptop to go the way of employer-provided health insurance: by 2017 less than half of the largest enterprises will still provide free computers with support to their employees. The other half will provide low-cost thin clients (smartphones, tablets, etc.) or offer a "technology credit" (as part of the growing BYOD trend).

Just as exciting are the wearables that are appearing with increasing frequency. Google Glass, Apple's iWatch, Plantronics' Bluetooth headsets, among countless do it yourself (DIY)–enabling devices, are changing the way we search, navigate, transact, and live. Chips can be implanted (inside of us) for all sorts of activities, and security and connectivity will be enabled by stomach acid–activated capsules we swallow, as appropriate.

Higher education is already thin. Undergraduate and graduate students live on their mobile devices. The pilots here should amplify the role that mobile devices (tablets, smartphones, etc.) play in the educational experience. For example, how much content can be delivered on smartphones versus tablets? Can smartphones replace tablets, which, as discussed above, are an integral part of many university content delivery strategies?

Wearables of all kinds should also be aggressively piloted. But is wearable technology really "ready?" This is the classic early adoption dilemma. If colleges and universities adopt too early, they will waste time and money; if they adopt too late they may lose competitive advantage. Remember that ready technology adoption is about piloting potential and discovering solutions to known and to-be-discovered problems. The wearable technology life cycle is just right: concepts are yielding pilotable prototypes. Colleges and universities should pilot the prototypes as soon as they are released.

As already discussed, wearables like Google Glass are already in pilots. Many of these pilots will dovetail with pilots that explore the *IOT and the IOE* that will change just about everything we think we know and do about mobility, search, transaction processing, and even personal relationship management. Fueling all this is the fact that within a few years the vast majority of Internet Protocol (IP) traffic will be driven by wireless devices.

The explosion of IP "identity cards" will enable personal business models and processes and the intersection of business and personal models and processes. Imagine when everything is addressable, accessible, and manipulable. Imagine when we can talk to and connect everything and every person on the planet. IOT/IOE is an infrastructure technology that will enable all sorts of imagined and unimagined activities. The more it spreads, the more activities it will support.

Higher education should pilot IOE/IOT across the board. It should extend its wearable technology pilots to connect with locatable books, buildings, automobiles, lab samples, and faculty, not to mention students. In fact, these pilots should involve wearables and location awareness driven by IOT/IOE.

Location awareness fundamentally alters business processes across multiple functional areas. The key is to define location-based services and discover the requirements that the technology can satisfy. For example, colleges and universities have a clear vested interest in knowing where their students and faculty are, both physically and virtually. They need to know the movement patterns of their "customers," and they need to correlate locations with a variety of attributes such as time of day, age, gender, wealth, and race, among other variables. The next step is to infer from that data precisely how to engage that customer with just the right communications and offers. Location awareness enables analytics.

The major consumer location-based platforms include Yelp, Neer, Loopt, SCVNGR, Gowalla, and Foursquare. These platforms enable a variety of activities and transactions and link to other social media sites to enable an "experience" that is both fun and monetizable.

The power of location-awareness and location-based services is growing. When combined with data about customer preferences, location-based services enable the real-time correlation of location-based marketing, selling, and service. Companies that touch customers with products and services should avail themselves to location-awareness and location-based services or they will find themselves at a competitive disadvantage to those who do. The relationship among analytics, social media, and location awareness is clear and cumulative. When integrated with mobility and cloud computing, the potential is even greater.

So if we look holistically at mobility, wearables, IOT/IOE, and location awareness, the number of higher education pilots is potentially huge. The mission of higher education could be enormously impacted by these and other ready technologies. In fact, the whole learning process could be made "continuous" by the technologies.

Imagine if students and faculty were continuously connected via mobile devices and location-awareness applications enabled by IOT/IOE. "Learning" would be mobile and "always on." The whole concept of timed/scheduled learning times would disappear in favor of push/pull learning models, where faculty would proactively communicate with students, and students would reactively collaborate with faculty and other students. The same students could proactively collaborate with other students and faculty in a continuous circle of communication and collaboration completely unconstrained by scheduled times or physical locations. This pilot would go way beyond online learning, which has tried its best to retain many of the old pedagogies and modes of delivery (for example, many online courses still meet at scheduled times).

The possibilities are endless. For example, imagine a marketing professor receiving an alert that several of his or her students are shopping (physically or online) at a store that is a great case study for a marketing principle discussed in class. The professor would be able to communicate with his or her students about the principle to students standing or virtually observing the principle in action. Similarly, location awareness could alert student teams of their virtual or physical proximity and prompt them to assemble to work on their joint project. The possibilities are endless.

Intelligent automation is the natural extension of artificial intelligence (AI) and expert systems design and development. It is also about the next generation of applications already appearing in horizontal technology architectures, like network and systems management frameworks, and in vertical applications, like those intended to make educators and educational administrators more effective. Many of these applications have some level of embedded intelligence.

Intelligent, automated systems will continue to routinize many decision-making processes. Rules about learning, management, resource allocation, and curricula administration will be embedded in automated applications. It is sure unlikely that individuals will go onto the Web and execute trivial transactions. Smart support systems will automatically execute hundreds of predefined, "authorized" transactions. There are expert system shells and templates that permit the design and implementation of automated transactions. There are off-the-shelf tools that support automation, though they are not always identified as important business process modeling applications. There are "rules" around processes and transactions that can be automated, as they already are within some (especially) retail transaction processing.

So let us assume that a student attempts to register for a course for which he or she is not allowed to register (because it is out of sequence or because the student has not had the necessary prerequisites). An intelligent system would immediately flag the conflict and suggest, and then enroll the student in, the correct course. Intelligent systems will manage all sorts of administrative and learning tasks and processes. *Examinations will be given by intelligent (software) agents.* Online and offline schedules will be managed intelligently by applications that learn from ongoing experiences. Some of the applications that enable intelligent activity are under development by third parties, but colleges and universities might also write their own applications using some of the widely available expert system shells.

In the 20th century, technology adoption in higher education was a slow, disciplined process. Most colleges and university CIOs, deans, and faculty were skeptical about what "new" technologies could actually deliver. Technology architectures and platforms were mainstream: Dell, Microsoft, WebCT, and so on. Colleges and universities obviously felt that technology was necessary, but they also believed that technology adoption should be very carefully managed.

Times have changed. As discussed throughout this book, the pace of technology change has dramatically accelerated. Higher education must track broad technology trends and specific ready technologies. The tracking/piloting/deployment of ready technology is a new core competency. Technology will continue to advance, and pilot/deployment delivery will continue to improve. The piloting and adoption of ready technology will become a competitive activity that colleges and universities will have to pursue. A new set of best practices will develop around ready technology tracking, piloting, and deployment. Agility and competitiveness will redefine themselves around ready technology.

Higher education should track technologies and technology-enabled business models. The industry has a variety of partners that help colleges and universities track trends and business process opportunities. One of these organizations is the New Media Consortium (NMC) that works closely with the EDUCAUSE Learning Initiative.[*]

NMC offers some thoughts about trends that colleges and universities should consider. The thoughts are also a rich source of ideas for ready pilots.

Here is a summary of their thoughts (*italics* added for emphasis by the author):

> Education paradigms are shifting to include online learning, hybrid learning, and collaborative models. Students already spend much of their free time on the Internet, learning and exchanging new information. *Institutions that embrace face-to-face/online hybrid learning models have the potential to leverage the online skills learners have already developed independent of academia.*

---

[*] See the New Media Consortium (NMC) Horizon Report: 2014 Higher Education Preview, December 2013 (http://www.nmc.org/publications/2013-horizon-report-higher-ed).

Social media is changing the way people interact, present ideas and information, and judge the quality of content and contributions. Educators, students, alumni, and even the general public routinely use social media to share news about scientific and other developments. The impact of these changes in scholarly communication and on the credibility of information remains to be seen, but it is clear that social media has found significant traction in almost every education sector.

The shift continues toward becoming a creator society. The Maker movement, user-generated videos, self-published eBooks, personalized domains, and other platforms have all seen steep increases in recent years. *Higher education is now in a position to shift its curricular focus to ensure learning environments align with the engagement of creator-students and foster the critical thinking skills needed to fuel a creator society. Courses and degree plans across all disciplines at institutions are in the process of changing to reflect the importance of media creation, design, and entrepreneurship.*

There is a growing interest in using new sources of data for personalizing the learning experience and for performance measurement. As learners participate in online activities, they leave a clear trail of analytics data that can be mined for insights. *Learning analytics is a collection of tools to process and analyze that data stream, and use it to modify learning goals and strategies in real time.*

There is a growing consensus among many higher education thought leaders that institutional leadership could benefit from agile startup models. Educators are working to develop new approaches based on these models that stimulate top-down change and can be implemented across a broad range of institutional settings. Pilots and other experimental programs can be developed for teaching and improving organizational structure, and then evaluated quickly using scientific methods.

Asynchronous voice and video tools are humanizing online learning. Historically, one of the major concerns people have expressed about online courses is the lack of interaction. People desire digital learning opportunities that mimic face-to-face experiences. Learning management systems and other services are beginning to incorporate recording features that allow both faculty and students to communicate more authentically online. For example, Canvas includes audio recording from text and Blackboard enables recordings that upload directly to YouTube. Media production and sharing are already inherent in a host of other free, easy-to-use social media platforms, such as Vimeo,

Instagram, and Vine. *Increasingly, faculty are creating videos for more than just lectures; they are using them as tools to introduce themselves, make announcements, and provide brief background or examples of assignments.*

Faculty training still does not acknowledge the fact that digital media literacy continues its rise in importance as a key skill in every discipline and profession. As lecturers and professors begin to realize that they are limiting their students by not helping them to develop and use digital media literacy skills across the curriculum, the lack of formal training is being offset through professional development or informal learning, but we are far from seeing digital media literacy as a norm.

New models of education are bringing unprecedented competition to the traditional models of higher education. Across the board, institutions are looking for ways to provide a high quality of service and more learning opportunities. *MOOCs are at the forefront of these discussions, enabling students to supplement their education and experiences at brick-and-mortar institutions with increasingly rich, and often free, online offerings.*

There are parts of the university enterprise that are at risk, such as continuing and advanced education in highly technical, fast-moving fields. *As online learning and free educational content become more pervasive, institutional stakeholders must address the question of what universities can provide that other approaches cannot, and rethink the value of higher education from a student's perspective.*

The flipped classroom refers to a model of learning that rearranges how time is spent both in and out of class to shift the ownership of learning from the educators to the students. After class, students manage the content they use, the pace and style of learning, and the ways in which they demonstrate their knowledge, and the teacher becomes the guide, adapting instructional approaches to suit their learning needs and supporting their personal learning journeys. Students can access this wide variety of resources any time they need them. *The flipped classroom model is part of a larger pedagogical movement that overlaps with blended learning, inquiry-based learning, and other instructional approaches and tools that are meant to be flexible, active, and more engaging for students. It has the potential to better enable educators to design unique and quality learning opportunities, curriculum, and assessments that are more personal and relevant to students' lives.*

Learning analytics is an educational application of "big data," a science that was originally used by businesses to analyze commercial activities, identify spending trends, and predict consumer behavior. Whereas analysts in business use consumer data to target potential customers and personalize advertising, *learning analytics leverages student data to build better pedagogies, target at-risk student populations, and assess whether programs designed to improve retention have been effective and should be sustained—outcomes for legislators and administrators that have profound impact.* For educators and researchers, learning analytics has been crucial to gaining insights about student interaction with online texts and courseware. Students are beginning to experience the benefits of learning analytics as they engage with mobile and online platforms that track data to create responsive, personalized learning experiences.

3D printing refers to technologies that construct physical objects from three-dimensional (3D) digital content such as 3D modeling software, computer-aided design (CAD) tools, computer-aided tomography (CAT), and x-ray crystallography.

The *games culture* has grown to include a substantial proportion of the world's population, with the age of the average gamer increasing with each passing year. As tablets and smartphones have proliferated, desktop and laptop computers, television sets, and gaming consoles are no longer the only way to connect with other players online, making gameplay a portable activity that can happen in a diverse array of settings. Gameplay has long since moved on from solely being recreational and has found considerable traction in the worlds of commerce, productivity, and education as a useful training and motivation tool. *The gamification of education is gaining support among educators who recognize that effectively designed games can stimulate large gains in productivity and creativity among learners.*

Quantified self describes the phenomenon of consumers being able to closely track data that are relevant to their daily activities through the use of technology. *The emergence of wearable devices on the market such as watches, wristbands, and necklaces that are designed to automatically collect data are helping people manage their fitness, sleep cycles, and eating habits. Mobile apps also share a central role in this idea by providing easy-to-read dashboards for consumers to view and analyze their personal metrics.*

As *voice recognition and gesture-based technologies* advance and more recently, converge, we are quickly moving away from the notion of interacting with our devices via a pointer and keyboard. *Virtual assistants* are a credible extension of work being done with natural user interfaces (NUIs), and the first examples are already in the marketplace. The concept builds on developments in interfaces across the spectrum of engineering, computer science, and biometrics. *The Apple iPhone's Siri and Android's Jelly Bean are recent mobile-based examples that allow users to control all the functions of the phone, participate in lifelike conversations with the virtual assistant, and more.*

A new class of *smart televisions* are among the first devices to make comprehensive use of the idea. *While crude versions of virtual assistants have been around for some time, we have yet to achieve the level of interactivity seen in Apple's classic video, Knowledge Navigator.* Virtual assistants of that caliber and their applications for learning are clearly in the long-term horizon, but the potential of the technology to add substance to informal modes of learning is compelling.

There are other interesting trend analyses, like the following from Ellyssa Kroski, who validates some of the NMC trends and identifies some new ones[*]:

3D Printers which enable makers to create whatever they can imagine and design have exploded into mainstream culture over the past year.

Libraries are creating DIY makerspaces and providing these new tools of production to their communities along with opportunities for skill-building in math and engineering which are required to design 3D objects. And schools are not far behind, realizing the many educational possibilities of the devices. *The Poland and Hong Kong based GADGETS3D has launched an initiative called the "3D Printer in Every School" project in which they have designed a low-cost, small 3D printer specifically created for the classroom.*

MOOCs or massively open online courses have exploded in popularity over the past two years and will continue to grow over the next several. These (usually) free courses are attended by hundreds of thousands of students at the same time and offer both certificates of completion and occasionally college credit. Online students can learn anything from basic computer skills to art history from Ivy-League

---

[*] Ellyssa Kroski, "7 Ed Tech Trends to Watch in 2014," December 23, 2013 (http://oedb.org/ilibrarian/7-ed-tech-trends-watch-2014/).

professors at well-respected institutions such as MIT, Harvard, Yale, Duke, and more. *I believe we will be seeing much more of these online courses in the coming years as they work out the kinks in the evaluation of large numbers of students and refine their focus. I think we will also start to see platforms dedicated to corporate MOOCs providing online training for businesses.*

Educational institutions, both higher ed and K-12, are making use of student data to improve classes, teaching methods, and entire programs. Just as businesses have been mining such data for years in order to predict trends and consumer behavior patterns, schools are now finding that such *"learning analytics"* will be effective in personalizing the educational experience for students at the individual level as well.

Digital textbooks replace the traditional print textbook with an eBook which is usually interactive and oftentimes open or free to use and sometimes edit. These new digital versions of classroom tomes have been undergoing pilot projects in K-12 classrooms for several years now.

According to a recent study by WeAreTeachers, *55% of the teachers surveyed use digital online games as part of their instruction, and 63% agree that students are more willing to practice difficult skills when presented in a game-like format.* Games-oriented labs and studios are popping up at universities such as the Game Studio at Boise State University, Pennsylvania State University's Educational Gaming Commons, Games Research Lab at Columbia University's Teachers College, and the Engagement Game Lab at Emerson College.

The Flipped Classroom is an active learning model which inverts the traditional method of providing instruction by providing video lectures for students to watch before class at home and activities and discussion in the classroom. This relatively new style utilizes online learning platforms such as Coursera and The Khan Academy to host video lectures and ed tech tools such as Show Me and Educreations to provide lessons via mobile whiteboards.

With the proliferation of tablets, smartphones, and other devices, educators have increasingly been embracing this new BYOD culture. They are using communication apps such as Twitter in classrooms, productivity tools such as Evernote, Dropbox, and Google Docs, digital textbook apps such as iBooks Author, video apps such as iTunesU, as well as apps specifically geared toward certain subject areas.

Finally, there are the trends presented by Davide Savenije who reports on trends identified by Lev Gonick, the vice president for Information Technology Services and CIO at Case Western Reserve University and CEO of OneCommunity[*]:

- Death of Personal Computers
- Proliferation of Mobile Devices
- Rise of Social Networks
- Next Generation of Networks
- Privatization of the Cloud
- Valuation of X-as-a-Service
- Promise of Big Data
- Implementation of the Flipped Classroom
- Future of the Learning Space
- Legitimization of Online Learning
- Evolution of the College Campus
- Advent of the Urban Operating System

These trends reflect current thinking on ready technologies and emerging learning processes. Note the overlap across the three lists, which suggest relative agreement on what is happening with higher education technology and technology-driven business models and processes.

Much of the technology is pilot ready. Ready colleges and universities should strategize proactively *and discover requirements reactively* through pilots designed to define and enable existing and whole new business models and processes. The higher education industry is changing quickly, and technology is driving the change. Much of the technology on the above lists is available for immediate pilots *because most of IT is third-party created, cloud delivered, and inexpensive.* Pilots can begin immediately.

But often the real obstacle to ready piloting is the culture in which pilot/no-pilot decisions are made. Many colleges and universities

---

[*] See Davide Savenije, "12 Tech Trends Higher Education Cannot Afford to Ignore," *Education Dive*, July 31, 2013, who reports on trends identified by Lev Gonick, the vice president for Information Technology Services and CIO at Case Western Reserve University and CEO of OneCommunity (http://www.educationdive.com/news/12-tech-trends-higher-education-cannot-afford-to-ignore/156188/).

are "ready," but many others are not. Higher education is often perfectly schizophrenic when it comes to technology adoption or even technology investments of any kind. This is often because there is ongoing financial pressure to keep technology (and other) costs as low as possible (even if ready technology deployment might save lots of money).

Delays may also be attributable to the not-for-profit syndrome. Higher education pursues the greater good; it does not exist to make money (though it actually needs to). The industry's competitive pressures are varied and segmented. For example, many state colleges and universities compete primarily with other state colleges and universities, not with private institutions. Similarly, small liberal arts schools often compete only with other small liberal arts schools, not large state schools or even larger private colleges or universities. Some schools specialize in engineering or business: the Wharton School of the University of Pennsylvania seldom competes with Carnegie-Mellon's engineering programs. So the competitive drivers of change are more complicated than the competition between Target and Wal-Mart.

Finally, higher education has many younger but many more older faculty, which complicates the change equation. Where younger faculty are quick to adopt new technology and technology-enabled pedagogy, older faculty often resist change, particularly technology change. Many ready technology pilots in higher education thus often have split support. Administrators are sensitive to faculty demographics, especially since many of the older faculty have tenure.

All of this speaks directly to "readiness." Some industries are more likely to pilot new technologies than others. Higher education has natural curiosity and student demand offset by budget constraints, demographics, and customer segmentation. The discussions in Chapters 3 and 4 about ready processes and companies should inform our understanding of technology readiness and the likelihood of technology piloting. Ready technology processes are inherent in some industries and companies, but very definitely something that must be learned by others. Higher education would probably earn a *B* or maybe a *B+* in technology readiness, but not an *A*.

Retail

Now turn to the retail industry (which earns a solid *A* in technology readiness).

Retail has changed fundamentally over the past decade. Arguably Amazon.com redefined how we shop for just about everything. Just about every retailer on the planet is online. The retail industry has availed itself of countless technologies and business models and processes defined/enabled by IT.

How might ready technologies enhance the processes they already support?

What new processes might be defined and supported?

Let us look at the same technology clusters discussed in Chapter 1 (and discussed above with regard to higher education):

- Cloud
- Architecture
- Social Media
- Big Data Analytics
- BYOD
- Interfaces
- Thin and Wearable Devices
- IOT/IOE
- Location-Based Services
- Automation

How can the retail industry exploit these ready technologies?

One of the major strengths of *cloud computing* is the freedom it provides companies, *and retailers specifically,* to think operationally and strategically about how they want to leverage digital technology. Instead of worrying about network latency and server maintenance, technology retailers can focus on innovation, sales, and marketing, among other activities (within and beyond the cloud). Scalability is often just a phone call, e-mail, or alert away: it does not matter how many customers are online or in stores. The freedom from software maintenance, denial-of-service attacks, software version control, viruses, backup, and recovery, and other academic operational headaches is provided by cloud computing (assuming, of course, that the cloud provider is competent).

Retailers already exploit all kinds of cloud services. Retailers can move (and have already moved) massive amounts of operational and strategic technology to the ready cloud. There is no reason for retailers to run their own computing and communications power plants, though some, like Amazon, do.*

Ubiquitous cloud delivery has permeated the entire retail industry. Continuous pilots might consist of a suite of cloud providers. The pilots might measure the effectiveness, reliability, and security of alternative cloud providers, among other performance metrics. In other words, even though retailers may already have selected their preferred cloud providers, they should continuously pilot the offerings of other providers.

Distributed architectures, APIs, and software components are yielding rapid-active versus slow-passive software design. Instead of rigid, embedded processes, active software architectures enable the addition or subtraction of functionality through component architectures and APIs that will grow increasingly flexible and available from a variety of sources including the original authors of the software and all kinds of software mercenaries. Open-source APIs make it possible to reengineer functional designs in near real time. Software can be designed in interoperable pieces, not monolithic structures. APIs and other components will enable functional interoperability, extensibility, and adaptability. The integration of disparate cloud delivery technologies is also part of the trend toward architecture compatibility, which is extremely important to the adoption of ready technology.

All of this can be exploited by retailers. Amazon has done an incredible job exploiting existing—and developing their own proprietary—APIs. In fact, there is an ongoing API battle among retailers and other product/service providers.[†]

App stores represent a whole new software development and distribution channel, and retailers can continuously avail itself of these apps. The cost of developing and piloting new apps is minimal.

---

* Amazon supports itself (see http://highscalability.com/amazon-architecture). It also offers cloud services to a variety of customers, including Netflix, through its Amazon Web Services (AWS) offerings (see http://aws.amazon.com/).

† Lyman, Jay, "The Great OpenStack-Amazon API Debate," *LinuxInsider,* August 8, 2013 (see http://www.linuxinsider.com/story/78672.html). Also see Sony Priya, "The API Wars Are Coming," *The Enterprise Integration Zone,* December 3, 2013 (see http://java.dzone.com/articles/api-wars-are-coming).

As discussed, social media is everywhere. *Social business intelligence* is the goal for every company with customers. The intersection of traditional structured data and unstructured social data (from Facebook, Twitter, YouTube, forums, and blogs) represents opportunities for next-generation business intelligence and predictive analytics. The billions of posts, tweets, and blogs every month represent the richest communications and collaboration channel in history. Retailers have already developed formal *and permanent* social media listening and analysis strategies. As they all know, it is important to explore the options and weigh the results against a set of listening/analysis/engagement goals (which, ideally, are derived from an explicit retail social media strategy).

What are customers saying about Wal-Mart, Amazon, and Target? What are the good tweets and the bad ones? What are the trends? Who are the social "influencers"—the tweeters and bloggers that many people listen to week after week?

Retailers want to understand what everyone and anyone says and thinks about their products, services, and brand. They need to understand customer motivations and concerns. They need to know what they like and dislike, and they need to know this continuously and ideally in real time. Changing social media listening vendors presents no special problems. Changing the listening/analysis parameters does not present special problems: retailers can change when/where/how they listen/analyze with an e-mail (or text message, or even a tweet). The social media listening marketplace is very competitive.

Retailers should avail themselves of ready social media technology to enable the following:

- Market Research
- Brand Management
- Competitive Intelligence
- Product/Service Innovation and Life Cycle Management
- Customer Services

The *real-time big data analytics* challenge is real and growing. "Data" are no longer owned by the enterprise. Data are created by anyone who would like to offer insights, solve problems, buy products and services, or just complain.

The end-game for retailers is simple: real-time descriptive, explanatory, predictive and prescriptive data, information, and knowledge about internal and external processes and performance. But there are challenges. The amount of data streaming into retailers is huge and growing.

The power of analytics is clear: the more descriptive, explanatory, predictive, and prescriptive insight a retailer has, the better its operational and strategic performance. The ability to observe and tune operations and strategy, especially in real time, is essential to competitive positioning and growth. Analytics is awareness and engagement. Retailers that ignore analytics will weaken their ability to compete.

Most of these are strategic questions that demand timely answers. The technologies that generate the answers include standard DBMSs and tools designed specifically for structured and unstructured big data analytics, such as Hadoop, which should be installed and used to ask and answer the above kinds of questions. Hadoop is far from perfect, but it is ready. All of the large retailers already have elaborate DBMS platforms in place, as well as sophisticated analytics engines. Analytics is a new and permanent retail industry core competency.

BYOD is already at work. We are all familiar with the model. Employees, suppliers, and partners are encouraged to use whatever digital devices they prefer while working in, or interacting with, your company. Some believe that the BYOD movement is about reducing corporate technology expenses, while others believe that happy employees/suppliers/partners are productive employees/suppliers/partners. It is a fast-moving trend that is uncovering many issues that companies and their technology providers are quickly addressing.

Like all industries, the retail industry is piloting BYOD. As part of their larger IT strategies, retailers are assessing the strengths and weaknesses of the BYOD delivery model for their employees and partners. (Obviously, BYOD takes on a completely different meaning for retail customers, where they use whatever devices they want to access retail Web sites.)

The interfaces we use to interact with hardware and software of all kinds are changing. Speech input is becoming more capable, and other interface technology like gesture control is also gaining momentum. Displays are becoming more interactive and intuitive: "visualization" was impressive in the 1990s, and today it is essential and intelligent.

Biometrics are now, after many years, moving mainstream. While there were deployments of biometric technology in selected industries and for specific purposes, smartphones have consumerized biometric authentication. Facial recognition technology (and other biometric interfaces) is also advancing at a rapid pace. Such technology will facilitate access to, and other "controls" of, devices, processes, and transactions that retailers can use.

Thin and wearable is definitely here. Most of us access the Internet with a "thin" device. Increasingly, these devices are on or even in us. While we still use desktops and laptops, increasingly we use tablets, smartphones, and other thin clients to access local area networks, wide area networks, virtual private networks, the Internet, hosted applications on these networks, as well as applications that run locally on (some of) the devices. The economics are so compelling for thin clients that we can expect the "fat" corporate PC and the venerable laptop to go the way of employer-provided health insurance: by 2017 less than half of the largest enterprises, including retailers, will still provide free computers with support to their employees. The other half will provide low-cost thin clients (smartphone, tablets, etc.) or offer a "technology credit" (as part of the growing BYOD trend).

Just as exciting are the wearables that are appearing with increasing frequency. Google Glass, Apple's iWatch, Plantronics' Bluetooth headsets, among countless DIY-enabling devices, are changing the way we search, navigate, transact, and live. Chips can be implanted (inside of us) for all sorts of activities, and security and connectivity will be enabled by stomach acid–activated capsules we swallow, as appropriate.

The retail industry is already "fat" and "thin": customers can conduct online transactions pretty much with any digital device they have. The industry enables transaction processing anywhere and everywhere, physically and virtually. Digital technology is the lifeblood of the retail industry. It must "work," and it must improve every year.

Customers live on their mobile devices. The pilots here should amplify the role that mobile devices (tablets, smartphones, etc.) play in the retail experience. For example, how much content can be delivered on smartphones versus tablets?

Retailers should also aggressively pilot wearables. But is wearable technology really "ready?" This is the classic early adoption dilemma. If retailers adopt too early they will waste time and money; if they adopt too late they may lose competitive advantage. Remember that ready technology adoption is about piloting potential and discovering solutions to known and to-be-discovered problems. The wearable technology life cycle is just right: concepts are yielding pilotable prototypes. Retailers should pilot the prototypes as soon as they are released. For example, can Google Glass users be permitted to talk to Wal-Mart's products, buy them, and return items that break? Wal-Mart applications will enable Glass transactions. There will be numerous wearables that Wal-Mart and other retailers (and third parties) enable.

Many wearable pilots dovetail with pilots that explore the IOT and the IOE that will change just about everything we think we know and do about mobility, search, transaction processing, and even personal relationship management. Fueling all this is the fact that within a few years the vast majority of IP traffic will be driven by wireless devices.

The explosion of IP "identity cards" will enable personal business models and processes and the intersection of business and personal models and processes. Imagine when everything is addressable, accessible, and manipulable. Imagine when we can talk to and connect everything and every person on the planet. IOT/IOE is an infrastructure technology that will enable all sorts of imagined and unimagined activities. The more it spreads, the more activities it will support.

Retailers have already piloted first-generation IOT/IOE. Many of their products have implanted chips and communications links. Refrigerators talk to grocery stores and clothes talk to cleaners. Retailers can know where their products are and how they are being used. They know when products malfunction and when they need to be upgraded (enabling cross-selling and upselling—what every retailer loves).

Location awareness fundamentally alters business processes across multiple functional areas. The key is to define location-based services and discover the requirements that the technology can satisfy. Retailers have a clear vested interest in knowing where their customers physically and virtually are. They need to know the movement patterns of their customers, and they need to correlate locations with a variety of attributes such as time of day, age, gender, wealth, and race, among other variables. The next step is to infer from that data precisely how to engage that customer with just the right communications and offers. Location awareness enables retail analytics.

The power of location awareness and location-based services is growing. When combined with data about customer preferences, location-based services enable the real-time correlation of location-based marketing, selling, and service. Retailers that touch customers with products and services should avail themselves of location-awareness and location-based services or find themselves at a competitive disadvantage to those who do. The relationship among analytics, social media, and location awareness is clear and cumulative. When integrated with mobility and cloud computing, the potential is even greater.

Intelligent automation is the natural extension of AI and expert systems design and development. It is also about the next generation of applications already appearing in horizontal technology architectures, like network and systems management frameworks, and in vertical applications, like those intended to make educators and educational administrators more effective. Many of these applications have some level of embedded intelligence.

Intelligent, automated systems will continue to routinize many decision-making processes. It is sure unlikely that individuals will go onto the Web and execute trivial transactions. Smart support systems will automatically execute hundreds of predefined, "authorized" transactions. There are expert system shells and templates that permit the design and implementation of automated retail transactions. There are off-the-shelf tools that support automation, though they are not always identified as important business process modeling applications. There are "rules" around processes and transactions that can be automated as they already are within some (especially) retail transaction processing.

Perhaps unlike the pace we see in higher education, technology adoption by retailers has been rapid and continuous. There is a small army of prognosticators that continuously discuss retail technology trends and, for our purposes here, identify a suite of ready pilots that retailers should launch.

Here is a summary of some thought leaders (*italics* added for emphasis by the author).

The first is from Neeraj Athalye, the head of sales for SAP's Platform and Technology Business. These thoughts appeared in *Information Week*[*]:

> Just 15 years ago, retailers were struggling to make sense of if and how the Internet would change their business. Fast forward to today, and the role that the digital world plays in shopping, dominates how retailers go to market and how consumers interact with brands. This one dynamic shift—*the rise of omni-channel buying*—is ubiquitous across every country that considers retail as core to its economy. Deloitte put it simply in its "Global Powers of Retailing 2013: Retail Beyond" report: "The retail paradigm has shifted from a single physical connection point with customers to a multipronged approach that crosses both physical and digital channels." Beyond this larger global trend, however, the shopping experience continues to evolve differently around the world. Some trends and innovations represent opportunities for retailers, others represent threats that require action in the form of anything from small adjustments—such as increasing accepted forms of payment—to a complete rethinking of the business model.
>
> *The balance of power has shifted in favor of the consumer who is now more in control than ever.* And retailers are left trying to understand the consumer mindset in this new omni-channel world; *how, when, why, and where consumers buy, what influences the purchase decision and channel, and how retailers can predict consumer demand.*
>
> Reimagining the in-store experience in the United States, *some retailers are turning toward an interactive "retailtainment" store model, which aims to deliver a customer experience that cannot be delivered online, with an emphasis on engaging and knowledgeable employees, in-store aesthetics, and interactive technology.* The open and monochromatic Apple stores—where consumers are encouraged to interact with products and engage with a staff of easily approachable "experts" and "geniuses"— served as a popular precursor for this model. In 2013, telecommunications giant AT&T launched its "Experience" store in Chicago that

---

[*] Neeraj Athalye, "How Emerging Technologies Are Transforming the Retail Industry Vertical," *InformationWeek*, December 6, 2013 (see http://www.informationweek. in/informationweek/perspective/286591/emerging-technologies-transforming-retail-industry-vertical).

eliminated the traditional store model in favor of a highly stylized, heavily digital store that puts an emphasis on face-to-face support and hands-on demos.

In the United States, nonelectronics retailers are using technologies such as touchscreen kiosks and digital signage to enhance the brick-and-mortar shopping experience. Staples, an office and home supplies chain, launched its first omni-channel stores in the summer of 2013 with "endless aisle" kiosks. These kiosks allow consumers to search for products in-store and online, and feature customer support tools, such as an ink-and-toner finder, to make shopping easier and more convenient. Macy's also is introducing in-store kiosks to its athletic apparel sections to better connect with consumers of the millennial generation that are accustomed to shopping online. *This combination of online ease-of-purchase with hands-on experience and the option of live customer service is an interesting twist on the in-store experience and one we are likely to see more of in the future.*

Tap and go payment technology has not yet been widely adopted in regions like Europe and North America, both retailers and consumers are embracing the technology "down under." Major Australian supermarket chain Coles conducts more than half its credit card transactions using contactless technology, which use *programs like Visa's payWave or MasterCard's PayPass and eliminate the need for consumers to enter a PIN or sign a receipt for purchases less than AUS$100.* Contactless transactions speed up the payment process as much as 25%, providing greater shopping convenience. It reduces cash-handling costs for retailers and can be integrated into rewards programs—eliminating the need to carry around physical punch or stamp cards—which can help drive customer loyalty.

Virtual Shopping South Korean workers annually rank among the top in the world for the number of hours worked per year, according to the Organisation for Economic Co-Operation and Development. So it should not be a surprise to hear of the success that Tesco's Homeplus grocery store chain found when it introduced virtual stores in the country's subway stations. These virtual stores are not "stores" in the true sense of the word. *Rather, they are printed graphics on subway walls that mimic a real store display, with a variety of products and brands stacked together just as they would be on a store shelf. Every item has a QR code for purchases. People can quickly scan the code to purchase their products, and the food will be delivered to their homes.* This form of shopping redefines what a convenience store can be, reducing the need for Korea's working population to take time out of their busy day for grocery shopping. It also helped Tesco Homeplus increase its online sales by 130%. *These smartphone-enabled stores are only in their infancy.*

Since launching the Korea virtual store, Tesco has expanded the concept to the U.K. COOP in Switzerland has also implemented remote scan and drive-through pick-up via its COOP@Home project. *In Canada, online health and beauty retailer Wells.ca and Walmart Canada have launched virtual stores.*

Retailers continue to innovate to provide more insight into consumers' buying habits and improve shopping experiences. Social media, for example, continues to be interwoven into people's lives, including shopping experiences. *Facebook recently began testing an online payment system that allows consumers to make online purchases from e-commerce partners through Facebook, which would allow shoppers to bypass the need to fill out billing information for every purchase.* And as online retailers strive to speed up delivery times, Google Shopping Express and Amazon are both launching efforts to provide same-day delivery.

New technologies will continue to evolve and improve shopping experiences at physical stores. *South Korean department store Shinsegae, for example, has created a virtual fitting room, in which a shopper gets a quick 3D body scan and can then view their avatar on a digital board wearing a full range of clothes available at the store.*

Swedish furniture giant Ikea is using augmented reality to allow consumers to visualize how furniture would look in their homes using only a smartphone app and the printed Ikea catalog. Consumers simply download the Ikea app and place the magazine wherever they want to see the furniture positioned on their mobile device. They can then select and manipulate different Ikea furniture, ensuring they find the right product, size, and color for their living space.

Some technologies—such as a new payment system that enables people to pay via an image of their face—will require consumer acceptance before they can be widely adopted. But retailers should always remember that being an industry leader or trendsetter requires a certain degree of risk taking. *They should also remember that using new technologies—or using existing technologies in innovative ways—can mean the difference between being an industry leader and being an industry follower in this highly competitive industry.*

These technologies suggest how the retail industry is adopting new technology at an incredible pace. The industry validates the argument here regarding the availability and readiness of new technologies that enhance the retail experience from browsing to paying. Retailers pilot and deploy quickly and continuously.

Another set of predictions from the *Retail Information Systems (RIS) News* appears below.* Again, *italics* are added for emphasis by the author:

"This year the retail industry will see major shifts take place, whether it is the convergence of online e-commerce with brick-and-mortar retailer, *the rise of digital currency like PayPal and Bitcoin at the checkout*, or the integration of wearable data to help consumers make smarter choices at the checkout," said Lisa Falzone, CEO of RevelSystems. "We are at the forefront of breakthrough technologies and believe the industry is headed towards a more integrated and user-friendly approach to retail."

"Industry advancements that will begin to take shape in 2014 include the following:

"Mobile and digital currency will go mainstream in retail. Mobile payment options will bridge people's online wallets with their physical ones at the checkout. People will be able to tap into digital currencies like PayPal, GoogleWallet and Bitcoin to pay for items at the checkout line. Smart-phones check calendars and geocentric data to offer you the best eating experience based on your schedule and preferences. POS terminals will act as beacons for the mobile consumer.

"CRM technologies will become 'smart' and predictive. Loyalty programs usually an afterthought to the POS, however, *by using smart peripherals such as facial recognition software*, a retailer's menu boards and POS displays can use predictive modeling based on past order history to recommend items for cross-sell and upsell opportunities.

"Social capital begins to influence personal pricing at brick-and-mortar. CRM systems will also include social data so that *more influential people over Twitter and Facebook can receive perks based on digital footprint and if they help publicize a business through checking-in or uploading products or establishments photos.* Offline and online experiences merge.

"Order-ahead features become the norm. Online and mobile ordering is standard, but with *order-ahead functionality, people no longer have to*

---

* See *Retail Information Systems News*, "Top POS Predictions for 2014," December 17, 2013 (see http://risnews.edgl.com/retail-trends/Top-POS-Predictions-for-201490104).

wait in line to make a purchase. This changes the nature of how retailers interact with consumers in restaurants, leading to more streamlined and intuitive ordering experiences.

"*Gamification will be offered in POS systems.* With the popularity of gamification technologies such as Yelp and Foursquare, POS systems will begin to *offer incentives like achievement badges and virtual rewards for both establishment owners and customers.* Retailers will have the potential to unlock achievements while customers can earn recognition."

John Foley of Oracle has a list of 10 technology trends that will revolutionize retail that is instructive—and suggestive of a variety of ready technology pilots (*italics* added for emphasis by the author)[*]:

Multichannel retail requires channel-synthesizing technology. At Oracle, we call this "commerce anywhere." Oracle Retail v14 supports processes that help customers buy, pick up, or return items via any retail channel and help retailers meet demand without constraints across those channels.

Analytics bring science to the art of retail. For years, retailers have managed some of the biggest data warehouses in the world. So they already have big data; now they must use those many terabytes to optimize operations, refine pricing, anticipate demand, and provide the product assortments customers want.

Mobility is much more than a smartphone app. Retailers can create a more seamless experience for customers, and increase the productivity and effectiveness of employees, by incorporating mobile technologies beyond smartphone shopping. For example, store employees can be equipped with tablets that have point-of-sale capabilities. And Tesco, one of the world's leading retailers, even introduced its own 7-inch tablet computer, the Hudl, which can be used for in-store shopping.

Visibility adds value to inventory. It is one thing to know that you have a pallet of product XYZ in a warehouse somewhere; it is much better to be able to tell your customer that XYZ is on its way and scheduled to arrive at a nearby store at 8 A.M. tomorrow. Retailers need comprehensive inventory planning, replenishment, and warehouse management capabilities, and they must be able to share the valuable information within those apps with customers.

---

[*] John Foley, "10 Technology Trends That Will Revolutionize Retail," *Forbes Magazine*, January 13, 2014 (see http://www.forbes.com/sites/oracle/2014/01/13/10-technology-trends-that-will-revolutionize-retail/).

Customer relationship management never gets easier. Customer relationship management (CRM) is a two-way street, but for retailers, it is a steady, and sometimes steep, uphill climb. Even if a customer is delighted when they leave your store (real or virtual), you have simply raised the bar of expectation higher for their next visit. This is why many CIOs and Chief Marketing Officers have begun thinking in terms of the customer experience, or CX, which includes a whole range of technologies and cloud solutions—including marketing and loyalty apps—that work in concert with a well-crafted CRM strategy.

Integration is everything. Multichannel retail must be seamless—for both retailers and customers—and that requires a level of systems and data integration that goes well beyond what most companies have in place. There are various reasons for that: online operations were originally established as a separate sales channel in many places; retailers have accumulated a mish-mash of special-purpose technologies for the Web, merchandise, and supply chain management, and so on; and mobile devices and social media create entirely new data streams. The good news is that not all data integration needs to happen in real time, which can be needlessly inefficient and expensive. The trick is to know where real time is essential and where it is not.

Your customers can (and should) be anywhere. Globalization represents a huge growth opportunity for retailers, but it is complicated, nuanced, and idiosyncratic, as different regions of the world have their own languages and currencies, fiscal and tax policies, and logistics challenges.

The transaction hinges on having the right product at the right time and place and at the best possible price. There is nothing new about this value proposition, but there is a lot new about how it is done. *Assortment planning, targeted assortments, life-cycle management of individual items, price optimization, markdowns, and inventory alignment are just some of the ways that retails can improve performance.*

Develop a strategy for showrooming. The popular practice of *showrooming*—where consumers go into a store to browse, then make lower-priced purchases online—is a cause of angst for the brick-and-mortar guys. But physical store retailers can fight back with real-time price matching and by equipping in-store employees with mobile technologies and information that puts them on an even keel with smartphone-carrying shoppers.

Go social, because you already are. In-store shopping is a highly social activity—it is face to face and we run into friends and neighbors while out and about. So it only makes sense that retailers would leverage social media to take full advantage of the customer engagement they already enjoy. *Retailers must plug into the social buzz, listen to customers, capitalize on what they learn, and use social tools and marketing best practices to build even better and more seamless customer relationships.*

The retail industry is a moving target that finds new technologies as quickly as the technologies find the industry. The synergism between retail and technology is complete. Operational technology, strategic technology, and, of course, ready technology are all in play as the retail industry reinvents itself almost quarterly.

Ready technology piloting is a permanent activity in the retail industry. The industry also utilizes the more traditional require-ments-first approach to technology adoption. In short, the retail industry is clothed in operational, strategic, and ready technology, and all flavors of diligence and deployment. The retail industry is also one of the biggest technology spenders, year after year, and as an unambiguously for-profit industry has every incentive to invest in technologies likely to reduce costs and increase revenue. The indus-try is also incredibly competitive, which also motivates companies to pilot technologies likely to give them a competitive advantage.

Healthcare

Let us look at the healthcare industry. Even the phrase *"healthcare industry"* is controversial. Is it an "industry?" Is healthcare a "business?" Or is it something else (around the world)? The United States has a for-profit healthcare industry that is designed to make a lot of money for providers, investors, and shareholders (of public companies, like Cigna [CI]). Without arguing the fine, and not-so-fine, points around for-profit healthcare businesses and healthcare effectiveness, an argument most Americans prefer to avoid,* there is a lot of oppor-tunity for providers to make even more money through the adoption

---

* The World Health Organization (WHO) listed the United States #37 (#46 in some other rankings) in healthcare delivery effectiveness in the world, but #1 in healthcare spending. For some inexplicable reason, this is the argument that most Americans never want to have (see http://www.huffingtonpost.com/2013/08/29/most-efficient-healthcare_n_3825477.html).

of ready technology. This, somewhat sadly perhaps, is the focus here.* (By the way, the healthcare industry earns a *B* in technology readiness.)

The U.S. healthcare industry has been an uneven user of information technology (IT) over the decades. On the one hand, many of the diagnostic procedures have benefitted from the latest IT, but on the other hand there have been incredible inefficiencies attributed to the slow adoption of electronic medical records (EMRs), a technology that is actually quite old. More recently, the U.S. government created some incentives for physicians and hospitals to adopt EMR technology, and some progress has been made, though the United States is way, way behind countries like Zambia,† Sweden, Denmark, and Finland, among countless others.‡

So how might ready technologies enhance and extend the processes they already support (or fail to support)?

What new processes might be defined and supported?

What are healthcare IT "best practices?"

Look at the same technology clusters discussed in Chapter 1 (and discussed above with regard to the higher education and retail industries):

- Cloud
- Architecture
- Social Media
- Big Data Analytics
- BYOD
- Interfaces
- Thin and Wearable Devices
- IOT/IOE
- Location-Based Services
- Automation

---

* I have the view that healthcare is a right and not a privilege. I do not believe that citizens should go bankrupt because they cannot pay their medical bills, or that care should be denied because of someone's inability to pay. In most industrialized nations, these are not issues at all, but in the United States—even with Obamacare—there are still problems with the cost and benefit of healthcare. Everyone should question the effectiveness of for-profit healthcare or at least alternative for-profit and not-for-profit healthcare delivery models or remain prepared to accept the consequences.

† http://www.jhpiego.org/content/zambia-leads-way-smartcare-electronic-health-records-system-benefit-both-providers-and-patie.

‡ http://www.nextgov.com/health/2009/09/us-lags-the-worlds-top-adopters-of-electronic-health-records-systems/44858/.

How can the healthcare industry exploit these ready technologies?

As oft-repeated here, one of the major strengths of *cloud computing* is the freedom it provides companies—*and healthcare providers specifically*—to think operationally and strategically about how they want to leverage digital technology. Instead of worrying about network latency and server maintenance, healthcare providers can focus on innovation, sales, and marketing, among other activities (within and beyond the cloud). Scalability is often just a phone call, e-mail, or alert away: it does not matter how many patients are online or in hospitals.

The freedom from software maintenance, denial-of-service attacks, software version control, viruses, backup, and recovery, and other academic operational headaches is provided by cloud computing.

Healthcare providers already exploit all kinds of cloud services. They can move (and have already moved) massive amounts of operational and strategic technology to the ready cloud. There is no reason for healthcare providers to run their own computing and communications power plants though some still do.

Ubiquitous cloud delivery has permeated the entire healthcare industry. Continuous pilots might consist of a suite of cloud providers. The pilots might measure the effectiveness, reliability, and security of alternative cloud providers, among other performance metrics. In other words, even though healthcare providers may already have selected their preferred cloud providers, they should continuously pilot the offerings of other providers.

The U.S. healthcare industry has some special legal requirements to which cloud providers must comply. Health Insurance Portability and Accountability Act (HIPAA) regulations are real and expanding. All technology providers must comply with HIPAA and related regulations.*

---

* "The HIPAA Privacy Rule provides federal protections for individually identifiable health information held by covered entities and their business associates and gives patients an array of rights with respect to that information. At the same time, the Privacy Rule is balanced so that it permits the disclosure of health information needed for patient care and other important purposes. The Security Rule specifies a series of administrative, physical, and technical safeguards for covered entities and their business associates to use to assure the confidentiality, integrity, and availability of electronic protected health information." (see http://www.hhs.gov/ocr/privacy/hipaa/understanding/summary/). Other countries have similar regulations (see "Health and Human Rights" the World Health Organization, http://www.who.int/hhr/en/).

There are also other sensitivities that define technology adoption and ready technology pilots. Privacy is always an issue as are perceptions about how the process works—that is, the relative roles of patients, doctors, nurses, drug manufacturers, and healthcare insurance carriers (and, of course, state and federal governments).

Distributed architectures, APIs, and software components are yielding rapid-active versus slow-passive software design. Instead of rigid, embedded processes, active software architectures enable the addition or subtraction of functionality through component architectures and APIs that will grow increasingly flexible and available from a variety of sources including the original authors of the software and all kinds of software mercenaries. Open-source APIs make it possible to reengineer functional designs in near real time. Software can be designed in interoperable pieces, not monolithic structures. APIs and other components will enable functional interoperability, extensibility, and adaptability. The integration of disparate cloud delivery technologies is also part of the trend toward architecture compatibility, which is extremely important to the adoption of ready technology. All of this can be exploited by the healthcare industry, which has a robust API community.*

App stores represent a whole new software development and distribution channel and retailers can continuously avail themselves of these apps. The cost of developing and piloting new apps is minimal. As more healthcare is delivered remotely via mobile devices, more healthcare applications will define healthcare delivery and management processes.

As discussed, social media is everywhere. *Social business intelligence* is the goal for every company with customers. The intersection of traditional structured data and unstructured social data (from Facebook, Twitter, YouTube, forums, and blogs) represents opportunities for next-generation business intelligence

---

* Charles Babcock, "Kaiser API Opens Healthcare Data to Mobile Apps," *InformationWeek*, June 3, 2013 (see Bottom of Form: http://www.informationweek. com/mobile/kaiser-api-opens-healthcare-data-to-mobile-apps/d/d-id/1110219). Also see Mark Braunstein, "Free the Data: APIs Boost Health Information Exchange," *InformationWeek*, January 27, 2014 (http://www.informationweek.com/ healthcare/electronic-health-records/free-the-data-apis-boost-health-information-exchange/d/d-id/1113579).

and predictive analytics. The billions of posts, tweets, and blogs every month represent the richest communications and collaboration channel in history. Healthcare providers have already developed formal and permanent social media listening and analysis strategies. As they all know, it is important to explore the options and weigh the results against a set of listening/analysis/engagement goals (which, ideally, are derived from an explicit higher education social media strategy).

What are customers saying about Cigna, Independence Blue Cross, and specific hospitals and doctors? What are the good tweets and the bad ones? What are the trends? Who are the social "influencers"— the tweeters and bloggers that many people listen to week after week? The healthcare industry is very active socially: there are sites where patients can assess their doctors, hospitals, insurance carriers, and pharmacies. Doctors get scored for their professionalism or lack thereof— some of the social commentary on specific physicians is brutal.

Healthcare providers want to understand what everyone and anyone says and thinks about their products, services, and brands. They need to understand patient motivations and their concerns. They need to know what they like and dislike, and they need to know this continuously and ideally in real time.

Healthcare providers—doctors, nurses, patients, insurance companies, pharmacies, drug manufacturers, research teams, the U.S. federal government, and U.S. state governments—should all avail themselves of ready social media technology to enable the following:

- Market Research
- Brand Management
- Competitive Intelligence
- Product/Service Innovation and Life Cycle Management
- Customer Services

The *real-time big data analytics* challenge is real and growing. "Data" is no longer owned by the enterprise. It is created by anyone who would like to offer insights, solve problems, buy products and services, or just complain.

The end-game for healthcare providers is real-time descriptive, explanatory, predictive, and prescriptive data, information, and knowledge about internal and external processes and performance. But there are challenges. The amount of data streaming into the healthcare system is huge and growing.

The power of analytics is clear: the more descriptive, explanatory, predictive, and prescriptive insight a healthcare provider has, the better the operational and strategic performance. The ability to observe and tune operations and strategy, especially in real time, is essential to competitive positioning and growth (remember, healthcare in the United States is a for-profit business). Analytics is awareness and engagement. Healthcare providers who ignore analytics will weaken their ability to compete.

Most of these are strategic questions that demand timely answers. The technologies that generate the answers include standard DBMSs and tools designed specifically for structured and unstructured big data analytics, such as Hadoop. All of the large providers already have elaborate DBMS platforms in place, as well as sophisticated analytics engines. Analytics is a new and permanent healthcare industry core competency.

BYOD is already at work. We are all familiar with the model. Employees, suppliers, and partners are encouraged to use whatever digital devices they prefer while working in, or interacting with, your company. Some believe that the BYOD movement is about reducing corporate technology expenses, while others believe that happy employees/suppliers/partners are productive employees/suppliers/partners. It is a fast-moving trend that is uncovering many issues that companies and their technology providers are quickly addressing.

Like all industries, the healthcare industry is piloting BYOD. As part of their larger IT strategies, the industry is assessing the strengths and weaknesses of the BYOD delivery model.

The *interfaces* we use to interact with hardware and software of all kinds are changing. Speech input is becoming more capable, and other interface technology like gesture control is also gaining momentum. Displays are becoming more interactive and intuitive: "visualization" was impressive in the 1990s, today it is essential and intelligent. Biometrics are now, after many years, moving mainstream. While there were deployments of biometric technology in selected industries, including healthcare, and for specific purposes, smartphones have consumerized biometric authentication. Facial recognition technology (and other biometric interfaces) is also advancing at a rapid pace.

Such technology will facilitate access to, and other "controls" of, devices, processes, and transactions that healthcare providers can use.

Thin and wearable is definitely here. Most of us access the Internet with a "thin" device. Increasingly these devices are on or even in us. While we still use desktops and laptops, increasingly we use tablets, smartphones, and other thin clients to access local area networks, wide area networks, virtual private networks, the Internet, hosted applications on these networks, as well as applications that run locally on (some of) the devices.

Wearables are appearing with increasing frequency. Google Glass, Apple's iWatch, Plantronics' Bluetooth headsets, among countless DIY-enabling devices, are changing the way we search, navigate, transact, and live. Chips can be implanted (inside of us) for all sorts of activities, and security and connectivity will be enabled by stomach acid–activated capsules we swallow, as appropriate.

The healthcare industry is already "fat" *and* "thin": patients communicate with pretty much any digital device they have. The industry enables transaction processing anywhere and everywhere, physically and virtually. Digital technology is quickly becoming the lifeblood of the healthcare industry. It must "work," and it must improve every year.

Patients live on their mobile devices. The pilots here should amplify the role that mobile devices (tablets, smartphones, etc.) play in the healthcare delivery experience. Note again that the devices must be HIPAA compliant.

Healthcare providers should also pilot wearables. The wearable technology life cycle is just right: concepts are yielding pilotable prototypes. Multiple healthcare applications will eventually enable Glass transactions. There will be numerous wearables that healthcare (and third-party) providers will enable.

Many wearable pilots dovetail with pilots that explore *IOT and IOE* that will change just about everything we think we know and do about mobility, search, transaction processing, and even personal relationship management. Fueling all this is the fact that within a few years the vast majority of IP traffic will be driven by wireless devices. IOT/IOE is an infrastructure technology that will enable all sorts of imagined and unimagined activities. The more it spreads, the more activities it will support.

Location awareness fundamentally alters business processes across multiple functional areas. The key is to define location-based services and discover the requirements that the technology can satisfy. Healthcare providers and patients have an obvious vested interest in knowing where everyone is. They need to know the movement patterns of patients, and they need to correlate locations with a variety of attributes such as time of day, age, gender, wealth, and race, among other variables. The next step is to infer from that data precisely how to engage that customer with just the right communications, for example, reminders about appointments, testing, and medications. Location awareness enables healthcare analytics.

The power of location-awareness and location-based services is growing. When combined with data about customer preferences, location-based services enable the real-time correlation of location-based healthcare delivery. The relationship among analytics, social media, and location awareness is clear and cumulative. When integrated with mobility and cloud computing the potential is even greater.

Intelligent automation is the natural extension of AI and expert systems design and development. It is also about the next generation of applications already appearing in horizontal technology architectures, like network and systems management frameworks, and in vertical applications like those intended to make educators and educational administrators more effective. Many of these applications have some level of embedded intelligence.

Intelligent, automated systems will continue to routinize many decision-making processes. It is unlikely that individuals will go on to the Web and execute trivial transactions. Smart support systems will automatically execute hundreds of predefined "authorized" transactions, like ordering medication. There are expert system shells and templates that permit the design and implementation of automated retail transactions. There are healthcare "rules" around processes and transactions that can be automated. As a "high-touch" field, healthcare can exploit automation in some important, even life-saving, ways.

Technology adoption by healthcare providers has at times been rapid and continuous but sometimes quite stilted. Nevertheless, there are countless opportunities for ready pilots. There are also a number of technology trends analysts who identify the technologies most likely to impact the overall healthcare process.

Here is a summary of some of their thoughts (*italics* added for emphasis by the author).

The first is from Karin Ratchinsky, the Director of Healthcare at Level 3 Communications. She blogs at BeyondBandwidth, where the following post originally appeared[*]:

> *Security:* Customer Data Services and IT Risk and Compliance companies alike predict that 2014 will be a year of headaches when it comes to data breaches for healthcare players. Experian notes that 46% of all breaches their data resolution department serviced in 2013 were healthcare related and that is expected to rise. Coalfire, an IT risk and compliance company, predicted that *healthcare IT breaches will be a* top 5 security theme *worry across all industries.* The proliferation of digitized PHI, lack of comprehensive risk mitigation strategies, recent omnibus rulings and increased audits all combine to create a hotbed for breaches in 2014. As a result, *focus will not only be on compliance but on IT risk management and process, including auditing and working with vendors to design and outline end to end security standards, expectations and responsibilities.*
>
> *The Year for Healthcare Cloud Adoption*: Healthcare has mismarked cloud as a security threat, when in fact many would argue that storing PHI remotely, perhaps in a private cloud, is far more secure than data locally stored on a laptop or memory key, the latter device being responsible for Kaiser Permanente's latest breach affecting 49K patients. *The HHS.gov site outlines that 69% of all individual cases affected by breaches have been from loss or theft of physical assets, 18% are from hacking or server theft, dispelling the idea that online theft lends itself to amplified breach numbers.* Shortly after the September Omnibus rule was passed, Amazon Web Services, the largest CSP announced they would be signing BAAs to satisfy the needs of the healthcare community. *More providers in 2014 will turn to the cloud to leverage a scalable, secure way to access and store data and HIT applications.*
>
> *Telemedicine*: Rectifying soaring medical costs is at the heart of nearly every HIT discussion and movement. Telemedicine has been proven as a cost effective, scalable and patient friendly way to connect the patient and care provider. According to the American Telemedicine

---

[*] Karin Ratchinsky, "Top HIT Trends for 2014: Accelerated Change Is Coming," January 16, 2014 (see http://www.healthcareitnews.com/blog/top-hit-trends-2014-accelerated-change-coming).

organization, 19 states have a working telemedicine parity policy and another 9 have a proposed law underway meaning soon more than half of U.S. states will compensate for telemedicine activities. *Providers can capitalize on a new type of revenue stream and realize other* telehealth *benefits.* A recent study from the UK's Department of Health outlines telehealth can bring about: 15% reduction in emergency room visits; 14% reduction in elective admissions; and 14% reductions in bed days. I have heard first-hand from CIOs and the numbers tell the same story, investing in telemedicine activities is a key priority.

Integration of Genomics and Predictive Modeling: The integration of genomics and predictive modeling is inevitable, so is the integration, in some fashion, into the EMR. This marriage is both highly exciting and overwhelming. Exciting because the correlations and intelligence that can be garnered from the now billions of digitized healthcare records is an unprecedented gold mine for research scientists and medical professionals alike. *This data can be harnessed to make more informed diagnoses and treatment decisions, recognize patterns in the greater population, and ultimately make our healthcare system more effective.* This movement is also highly overwhelming because of the amount and sensitive nature of this PHI. Nonetheless healthcare leaders as Mt. Sinai hospital in New York are taking the plunge with their $100 million commitment to integrate data and genomics into every aspect of their organization; the goal being to create more precise, positive patient outcomes. Although Mount Sinai is a true leader in this trend I predict we will see progress in 2014 driven by the proof that this type of intelligence improves care.

Empowering the Increasingly Demanding Patient: The message was clear at last week's digital health summit: *consumers want control over their health information.* Trends are showing that patients are increasingly looking for health information online including detail from patient portals. Frost & Sullivan estimates that patient portals will grow 221% through 2017. Empowering patients and holding them accountable is an essential part of improving care and consumers want access to information and tools that enable them to take such ownership. With health-related VC funding reaching unprecedented levels it is clear that this industry is ripe for innovation and providers need to get on board, harnessing technologies that deliver against patient expectations.

Another set of trends-based predictions comes from Neal Benedict, healthcare CEO at Verdande Technology.* Again, the *italics* are added for emphasis by the author:

> Over the past year, economic pressure and regulatory changes have increased scrutiny around areas of inefficiency within the healthcare industry. With new policies like the Affordable Care Act creating the need to improve patient outcomes and prevention, *2014 will be the year for much needed efficiency upgrades across the board at hospitals.* And with mounting pressure to cut costs amidst anticipated physician and other major shortages, new and innovative ways to leverage technology will be called upon to usher in changes for the healthcare industry.
>
> The business of care will continue to be a major area of focus for hospitals in 2014. Preventable, adverse events because of medical errors cost the healthcare industry more than $29 billion in 2013 and have led to between 50,000 to 100,000 deaths each year. *Healthcare professionals and hospitals cannot afford to continue accepting medical errors as balance sheet losses, which are not only jeopardizing profitability, but patient care.* To save money and improve patient care at the same time, hospitals will look to learn from technology being used successfully by other industries in 2014 *to enhance real-time analysis and, thereby, prevention and outcomes.*
>
> The Affordable Care Act had vast implications for the healthcare industry in 2013. Website issues aside, the increase in access will result in a number of new patients across the country. There are simply not enough physicians to handle this type of rapid growth, which will lead to concern over effective and comprehensive care. *In 2014, prevention technology will be necessary to help keep people out of hospitals.* By utilizing, for example, a system like *case based reasoning; physicians can work to prevent long term hospital visits for situations that could have been prevented at the early stages.*
>
> *Predictive analytics* have been used successfully within other industries, such as oil and gas, to help prevent nonproductive time that can save millions. By understanding what normal outcomes are the industry's historical data can be used to predict when an abnormal event,

---

* Neal Benedict, "2014 Health IT Trends: Technology Set to Tackle Inefficiency in Healthcare," *Electronic Health Reporter,* December 2, 2013 (see http:// electronichealthreporter.com/2014-health-it-trends-technology-set-to-tackle-inefficiency-in-healthcare/).

similar to one seen in the past, might occur. Despite the tremendous benefits *predictive analytics can provide for better decision management, the health-care industry has delayed adopting this approach, until now, for a number of reasons, including cost and legacy technology issues.* Clinicians lacked the tools available to manage and leverage healthcare big data needed for real-time decision-making, something that could greatly improve the risk for medical errors.

However, as awareness grows around predictive analytics, the approach has started to take hold in the healthcare industry as well. *The use of real-time analytics is also helping to improve transparency for administrators and patients around costs associated with procedures.* As this data is analyzed and the cases are built, alerts can be sent to both the hospital and to the patient about potential costs, helping to improve overall cost transparency and provide the data necessary for administrators and physicians to better make decisions. In 2014, adopting analytics techniques favored by the likes of Wall Street and major oil and gas companies will be necessary to make data backed decisions in real time and lower the risk for medical errors to improve the overall bottom line for hospitals.

Leveraging big data and predictive analytics in the healthcare industry has promise but what will be some of the techniques leveraged in 2014? With, for example, *Case-Based Reasoning (CBR) platforms, a large number of data on patient cases can easily be leveraged through a database to index past experiences and data on the situation and patient. The system can then use real-time data from the patient to continuously search the database for previous cases and risk profiles, enhancing the physician's ability to search for relevant cases with information they need to improve patient outcomes.* By providing an accurate assessment of whether a similar scenario is likely to occur on the operating table, CBR empowers clinicians with the evidence-based knowledge to make more comprehensive decisions improving patient outcomes.

By adopting these types of predictive techniques in 2014, the healthcare industry gains the opportunity to also prove to regulators that they are on the path to improving patient outcomes. This will help further demonstrate compliance and efficient patient management at hospitals.

The healthcare industry can no longer delay its adoption of efficiency based technology. The macro economic trends in 2013 have posed a number of challenges for the industry, though these challenges are creating the opportunity for a higher level of efficiency and cost cuts.

If physicians have historical reference support in real time, there can be an improvement of patient care and a higher level of efficiency that will stream-line efforts at hospitals.

ZDNet columnist, David Gewirtz, an IT advisor to the Florida Public Health Association, offers five trends worth considering (*italics* added for emphasis by the author)*:

1. The Continuing Growth of EHR

Electronic health record systems are finding their way into even the smallest doctors' offices and healthcare providers. *Within a year or so, we'll find almost universal EHR implemented within all facets of the health-care industry.*

The big question will be whether the EHR systems implemented (in some cases in a rush, and always on a budget) are *good* or not. *Healthcare providers will need to take care to do their due diligence in choosing EHR systems, or they may find themselves needing to rip-and-replace a few years down the road.*

2. Tablets Everywhere

It used to be that your doctor would tell you to take two tablets and call in the morning. Now, if when your doctor is talking about two tablets, she's most likely talking about iOS or Android devices.

In 2013, tablets will be used in more and more healthcare applications. They're small, portable, and relatively cheap. The issues that should concern healthcare providers are security and asset management. Many consumer-grade tablets can't provide the level of security required, so it may be a good idea to look towards vertically integrated Windows 8–based gear for many applications.

3. Pressure to Allow BYOD

Bring-your-own-device is a compelling opportunity for both employers and employees. Employees get to use the devices they want and like, and employers get to avoid paying for them.

But while BYOD has numerous challenges in "normal" organizations (including managing the variety of devices and compatibility issues), *BYOD can be particularly challenging in healthcare, when HIPAA*

---

* David Gewirtz, "Top 5 Healthcare IT Trends to Look Out for in 2013," *ZDNet Health,* December 27, 2012 (see http://www.zdnet.com/top-5-healthcare-it-trends-to-look-out-for-in-2013-7000009206/).

and HITECH regulations mandate particular care in ensuring that patient records don't leave when employees walk out of the building.

4. Vastly Increased Cybersecurity Threats Targeting Healthcare

Cybersecurity breaches are now all-too-common, but as the Washington Post reports, healthcare providers are particularly vulnerable to hackers.

This makes sense from a number of perspectives. First, more and more healthcare providers are entering the IT world because of new government regulations—and they're less than expert on how to do it. Second, healthcare is a huge industry with a lot of potential value to be stolen and scammed. *Beyond that, there are serious patient safety issues, and even the potential for blackmail.*

All in all, if cybersecurity doesn't get better in healthcare, we're going to be looking at a very unhealthy situation.

5. App-Enabled Consumer Tech

Mobile devices and smartphones are everywhere. We know this, because whenever we're out, there are legions of human-like creatures walking around, either staring into bright tiny screens, or holding them next to their heads, or seemingly mumbling into thin air.

A visitor from the mid-1990s would be shocked, and think we'd all been implanted by aliens or something, when, in fact, we've instead simply accepted the iPhone as our closest personal friend.

Many consumers are now doing all their Web surfing just on their phones, and many others—especially in developing countries—are gaining their first Internet access through the new low-cost smart-phones.

But a new trend has started to form: devices that derive their intelligence from smartphones, what are called app-enabled devices. Whether it's a healthcare monitor or a blood-pressure cuff, expect to see more and more of these in 2013. *If you're a physician, expect to start getting requests from your patients to directly access and evaluate their app-enabled device reports online.*

HP identifies some new areas and validates some others (*italics* added by the author for emphasis)[*]:

BYOD Is Becoming Mainstream. Don't Get Left Behind!

BYOD is becoming a necessity, and is now a real and manageable possibility for your employees who would like to be connected

---

[*] "Top 5 Healthcare Technology Trends for 2014" (see http://www8.hp.com/us/en/campaigns/healthcare/articles/2014-tech-trends.html).

to everything. The push for BYOD has reached a point that can no longer be ignored. Does your facility have a BYOD policy that is clearly defined and ready to embrace all types of devices, as well as operating systems? The IT infrastructure that enables BYOD needs to be addressed, as well as the governance and compliance issues such as establishing best practices that suit your organization. It is becoming imperative, and also much easier, to securely support the multitude of devices your doctors and support staff would like to use at work. *HIPAA compliance and security is always an issue, and certainly puts a strain on your IT department but the options for support are more readily available.* Hospitals and medical practices are starting to embrace the support requirements needed to enable their medical staff to bring their own devices to work, and not just allow usage on devices owned and managed by the medical facility. Expectations need to be met and policies put in place to manage confidentiality and privacy requirements, and be ready for the influx of new devices. The ROI for BYOD can still be hard to justify, but the payoff in terms of a happier, more productive staff will certainly contribute to a productivity increase. 2014 will see an increase in BYOD, and it is not going away, so this coming year may be a great time to embrace it.

Big Data Plays a Vital Role in Patient Care

We are seeing new phenomena where stored data is now accessible and useable. *Big data is being analyzed to gain valuable insights into ways to become more cost effective, and accelerate patient care. The focus has shifted to individual quality of care and increased access to relevant medical data enables a greater depth of knowledge.* As Electronic Health Records evolve, and are capable of working with outside apps, more relevant critical information is captured and recorded. *Data from all sources needs to be integrated for more efficient access, to help provide a more complete view for patient problems, diagnosis and treatment.*

Patients are also able to access their information from almost any device at any location. More hospitals and medical facilities are able to enter information into mobile devices and computers as it is obtained from the patient. The ability to combine all types of information entered through mobile devices increases the relevance of mobile technology. There is no longer a reason to avoid technology because it is perceived to get in the way of care. *Tablet computers can be taken into the consulting room, while many hospitals now have terminals outside each hospital room or a hub in the hallway with easy encrypted single sign on for all medical staff.* Access to comprehensive health data also enables more accurate prognosis and treatment decisions. Healthcare providers are realizing the benefit of big data and large-scale data analysis to deliver better care at lower costs as well as more customized treatment plans. There has been a resistance to change in the healthcare industry, but big data is playing a vital role that cannot be ignored. EHR systems are more affordable and information can be exchanged more easily than ever before.

Telemedicine Will Deliver Cost-Effective Care for the Future

Technology is cheaper and much easier to use and is continuing to push the envelope in terms of the options available to all patients, not just those who struggle to get to their medical facilities or hospitals. *Video conferencing through webcams on laptops and mobile devices means that patients can connect with their medical staff over the Internet with ease.* Receiving "virtual" care will continue to increase through 2014 and beyond. *Self-monitoring devices also make it easier for patients to monitor their own vital signs and report their information without having to make an appointment to see a medical care provider. Post hospitalization, patients can check in and upload their data, and the medical staff can videoconference with the patient or with other members of their team to monitor and consult through an interface that assists with HIPAA compliance.* Lack of reimbursement for treatment through telecommunications has been a barrier in the past; however, progress is being made from both political parties to change the requirements. Also using telemedicine to lower readmissions to hospital can help with Medicare reimbursement.

Data Security and Support Is Becoming Easier to Manage

Patient confidentiality and adhering to HIPAA requirements has become increasingly more challenging as IT continues to increase in complexity. *All personal health information must always be encrypted and the platforms that make this possible continue to evolve. The ability to erase information from devices that have been compromised has become a great backup tool.* Device tracking and wiping is now readily available as a security solution. Many hospitals have an internal team of IT support staff monitoring not only security, but also any IT emergencies, but there is more to be done to close the security gaps. Security products are available that provide secure leads for e-mail, texting and file sharing, as well as videoconferencing. It is imperative that mission-critical applications can continuously run with no concern about failures.

Mobile Apps Are on the Rise

Medical professionals rely upon their mobile devices to work effectively. They access mobile apps to quickly garner many types of information to make them more efficient. Patients use apps to monitor many aspects of their health, like counting calories, and measuring heart rate, to more complex regimens like managing chronic disease. Mobile apps will continue to be developed as they target specific needs. *This means innovative apps, especially within healthcare, are beginning to surface that can aid with more than just healthy lifestyle decisions, they will start monitoring more serious medical conditions. Medication adherence apps will help remind patients to take their medication through smart phone reminders. EHRs are also evolving with better usability to work with outside apps for data input and monitoring.* Health systems are developing and implementing their own apps to help improve the patient experience. Apps are being developed to span many different devices, and will play a vital role in healthcare now and in the future.

As technology continues to develop at a dramatic pace, we will see an increase in the use of many types of electronic devices and a drop in paper based note taking within the healthcare environment. *The further development of products and services such as touch based convertible tablets, servers, cloud computing, smart machines, and smart printers will encourage a major technology shift in hospitals and medical facilities throughout the world.* We will also see an increased push in cost reduction initiatives in order to advance the progress related to the vital task of improving patient outcomes.

The conundrum of U.S. healthcare IT continues. The opportunities are endless. Patients and their providers can digitally connect and manage treatments of all kinds. Wearables represent an obvious way to collect and communicate patient information. Telemedicine is another easy way to connect patients with their providers. Thin client—smartphone/tablet—applications can revolutionize the delivery of all kinds of healthcare services. Like the higher education and retail industries, healthcare can be transformed with current, emerging, and ready technology. It would be easy to identify 10, 20, or even 50 ready technology pilots.

But there are obstacles that, as with the higher education industry, constrain ready piloting. Some of these constraints, like HIPAA, are understandable, but others are not: there is a "cultural" predisposition against the wide-scale digital transformation of the healthcare industry in spite of lip service to the contrary. So we are left with an agenda without a manager. Over time, of course, ready pilots with launch and ready technology will be deployed. But the process will be painful.

The three industries discussed here are all ready technology candidates. In fact, it is hard to find an industry that is *not* ready. The discussions about each of the industries reveal a lot of synergism and a lot of uniqueness. The technology companies that create the technologies and assist in their piloting and deployment win horizontally *and* vertically. The extensibility of their products and services is complete. Plus, they get to customize their technology solutions around specific industries and companies.

The pace of technology change, and the maturity of out-of-the-gate technologies, creates ready technology opportunities. Higher education, retail, and healthcare benefit from fast/mature technologies. While other things must be true for widespread exploitation of ready opportunities, there is more than enough momentum to justify the ready philosophy in these three, and many other, industries.

6
CONCLUSIONS

Ready technology is real *and* perceived. Many of today's new technologies are more than ready for deployment. But many managers and executives believe that the adoption of new technology is inherently risky. The ready argument made here assumes some major differences between the old, "emerging" technology and ready technology. These differences should be explored and discovered through pilots designed to measure the contribution these technologies can make to business problem solving.

The old technology adoption process is predicated on technology capability. The conventional assumption is that technology *evolves* at a pace that justifies *phased* adoption. Early deployments are assumed to be risky but have a *potentially* high payoff, because the technology is likely not fully baked. Later adoption is safer, especially if a company is part of the "early" or "late" majority and has prior experience that justifies the approach to technology adoption.

The old adoption process also assumes up-front requirements due diligence where business requirements are well understood and well defined before candidate technologies are vetted. The essence of this approach is *requirements first/technology second*. It all made sense back then and aspects of the requirements-first/technology-second adoption model still make some sense today.

But things are also different now: there are immediate business opportunities that ready technologies present to even the most conservative technology adopters. Some of these "opportunities" are relatively well understood, while others are to be discovered (TBD). *What this means in practice is that a specific technology, or even a basket of technologies, may well be adopted without any specific problems in mind.* The assumption is that technologies like tablets, social media, and analytics will quickly solve some problems, even if the problems are unclear *or even unknown* at the time of adoption.

The approach assumes that technologies should drive requirements, and not the other way around, which is why ready technologies are "discovered" through deployment versus defined before technologies are deployed. As suggested, in Chapter 1, Marchand and Peppard (2013) make the same case regarding analytics projects. They describe what they call *"discovery-driven project management"* as comprised of the following steps:

- Develop Theories
- Build Hypotheses
- Identify Relevant Data
- Conduct Experiments
- Refine Hypotheses in Response to Findings
- Repeat the Process

They argue that successful technology deployments are discovered, not managed, and that companies should "experiment" with technologies until they find the right combination of requirements and technologies, *which is the essence of the ready argument made here.*

Operational technology can be "ready"; strategic technology can be "ready." Ready technology is deployable quickly and cheaply. Ready technology is technology that has achieved a level of maturity that makes it operationally or strategically ready for business, even if the details of the requirements are poorly understood.

Ready technology is emerging technology on steroids. *The major distinctions between emerging technology and ready technology include (a) the length of the due diligence process, (b) the importance of early requirements validation, and (c) fundamental assumptions around the technology adoption process itself, among some other differences that present opportunities to improve business processes very quickly and very cheaply.*

In fact, ready technology is *ready* because it is

- Out-of-the-Gate "Mature"
- Requirements Agnostic
- Usually Delivered from the Cloud
- Fast and Cheap
- Risk Neutral

Ready technology challenges 20th century technology adoption models that were (and still are) so popular among technology buyers, especially traditional technology buyers in large organizations. If we look at the adoption of iPads, social media, and BYOD alone, for example, we see much earlier, almost instant, technology adoption rates. In fact, it was reported *that 93% of Fortune 100 companies adopted iPads immediately after they were introduced.*[*] Obviously the professionals and companies that adopted all these iPads did not take a lot of time to vet, publish, and validate a long list of unambiguous business requirements.

The list of ready technologies will continue to grow. The 10 clusters discussed here will be piloted and deployed and then followed by an ever-changing set of technologies ready, willing, and able to go to work.

A commitment to watching and researching emerging technologies and adding them to the ready list should become a core competency. The power of ready technologies and their potential to change the way your company does business is wide and deep. Given how relatively inexpensive the technologies are to pilot and deploy, there is enormous leverage in the development and implementation of a ready strategy. You can count on your vendors, employees, customers, suppliers, and partners to help you exploit ready technologies.

Today, many emerging technologies are ready for immediate deployment. Ready technology is accessible and cost-effective. It also often arrives at companies without the participation of the corporate IT team, especially in federated or decentralized companies where business units and employees are encouraged to solve their own problems. Why is it so pervasive? And sticky? Because a lot of ready technology is consumerized, cheap, and easy.

Technology has fully democratized over the past five years; IT departments have relatively little influence over what employees download, use, and share. The sharing process is especially important to understanding why ready technology spreads. When one or two professionals decided to make Dropbox their virtual disk drive, and started to store all sorts of data on that drive, others had no choice but to participate. The more senior the initial adopters, the faster the ready technology got "shared."

Figure 6.1 summarizes *defined* and *ready* technology adoption and the *implications* of ready technology adoption.

---

[*] Apple reported that 93% of Fortune 500 companies have deployed or are testing iPads (see http://venturebeat.com/2012/01/04/ipad-enterprise-it/#sZBVhhB7uxj1vk4U.99).

Defined Adoption	*Ready* Adoption	Implications	Examples
• Defined Business-Driven Requirements Analysis and Validation • Full Technology Pilot Demonstrations Prior to Deployment • Required Integration of New Technology into Existing Technology Architectures • Transition Period to Test and Integrate New Technology • Continuous Support and Refresh Requirements	• Defined and Undefined Consumer-Driven Requirements Analysis and Exploration • Uncontrolled, Ad Hoc Technology Pilots • Limited or No Integration of New Technology into Existing Technology Architectures • Immediate Adoption and Delivery through Cloud Providers • Limited Support and Refresh Requirements	• Accelerated Technology Adoption • Increase in "Fail Fast/Fail Cheap" Pilots • Rapid Technology-Driven Business Process Change • Improved Technology TCO/ROI, Especially through the Avoidance of Large Integration, Support, and Refresh Costs • Major Changes in Corporate Governance of Information Technology	• BYO: Devices, Applications, Data, etc. • Tablets (such as iPads) • Smartphones (such as iPhones and Androids) • Content/File Sharing (with, e.g., Dropbox) • Mobile Applications (from App Stores) • Social Networking (with Facebook, Twitter, Flickr, etc.) • Video-Teleconferencing (with Facetime, Skype) • Video Sharing and Marketing (with YouTube) • Location Awareness (with, e.g., Foursquare)

Figure 6.1   *Defined* versus *Ready* technology adoption.

There are a variety of ready technologies already at work solving a variety of problems across multiple vertical industries.

The new governance process is significant because it often bypasses corporate information technology (IT) and the policies and procedures aligned to specific vertical industries, like manufacturing, pharmaceuticals, and financial services. In fact, every industry is ready, though must keep compliance and security in mind as it officially, *or unofficially*, adopts new technology.

At Shire Pharmaceuticals, for example, ready technology found its way into the trenches through the C-Suite: *Shire professionals adopted iPhones, iPads, Skype, ListenLogic, and Dropbox before corporate IT could assess their reliability, security, or total cost of ownership (TCO)/return on investment (ROI).* But everyone got to keep their iPads (and other toys) when IT ultimately declared them "safe," *well after their deployment.*[*] Similar events occurred at Balfour Beatty, Luxottica, and RehabCare.[†]

---

[*] There are lots of stories about how iPads found their way into the enterprise without the approval of corporate IT departments. See Tom Kaneshige, "iPads in the Enterprise: IT Must Stay Ahead of the Curve," *CIO Magazine,* May 1, 2012 (http://www.cio.com/article/705379/); Sean Ludwig, "The iPad Is an Incredible Tool for Work—If Your IT Department Will Allow It," *VB Mobile,* January 4, 2012. The Shire case is documented in Stephen J. Andriole, "The Transformation of Technology at Shire Pharmaceuticals," the Acentio Group, December 2012.

[†] See Matt Rosoff, "Huge Construction Firm Uses iPads and Apple TV to Save Millions," *CITEWORLD,* March 28, 2013; Ludwig (http://venturebeat.com/2012/01/04/ipad-enterprise-it/2/).

The same process is playing out in banks, consultancies, higher education, retailers, and the healthcare industry. *In fact, there is no way to stop the process, as many companies discovered when they tried to ban social networks.**

The deployment of iPads, social media, file sharing, and video-teleconferencing (among other technologies) at Shire and other companies demonstrates just how fast technology can be adopted.

The rapid adoption of *social media listening technology* is another example. Once it was possible to listen to all varieties of social conversations, companies quickly found listening partners (like ListenLogic and Radian6 [now part of salesforce.com]), and started mining social data about what their customers liked and disliked about their products and services.

Dropbox is cloud file sharing. Countless professionals use Dropbox to store and share files of all kinds. Skype and Facetime are ready technologies used extensively for collaboration and communication, even at companies with expensive proprietary video-teleconferencing (VTC) systems. App stores are not the stores of last resort, but often the first stores visited by professionals with problems to solve. Mobile application development is also exploding. Foursquare is ready for location-based services, and YouTube is for video sharing for training and marketing.

The first implication of ready technology adoption is speed. Ready technology adoption immediately unleashes the power of new technology. Put another way, ready technology adoption, as chaotic as it sometimes is, enables us to "fail fast/fail cheap" and redefines the whole "piloting" process. It also enables rapid business process modeling (BPM) by introducing new capabilities applied to old processes, like how we collaborate through cloud file sharing (Dropbox) or how we see each other while traveling (Skype, Facetime). But perhaps the

---

* See Jacques Bughin and Michael Chui, "How Social Technologies Are Extending the Organization," *McKinsey Quarterly*, April 2011 (http://www.mckinseyquarterly.com/Business_Technology/How_social_technologies_are_extending_the_organization_2888). Also see: "54% of Companies Ban Facebook, Twitter at Work," *Computerworld*, October 6, 2009; Kim Bhasin, "Companies around the World Are Banning Social Media Sites at Work More Than Ever," *Business Insider*, September 6, 2011 (http://articles.businessinsider.com/2011-09-06/strategy/30128243_1_social-media-social-sites-software-security-firm#ixzz2R42rosQA).

largest implication of ready technology adoption is how it rearranges technology governance. In the 20th century, technology governance was centralized or federated. Ready technology adoption is federated, with a touch of pure decentralization. This means that employees/consumers in business units "govern" technology adoption and exploit what the technologies can provide without the "guidance" of corporate or business unit chief information officers (CIOs). This has profound implications for the acquisition and support of enterprise technology. For example, ready technologies enable business units to immediately acquire and deploy technologies without the customary due diligence that enterprise IT teams like to conduct. Similarly, since support is embedded in all cloud-delivered technologies, there is no "service/support" box for corporate IT to check-off or use as a barrier to adoption. In fact, the whole notion of "enterprise technology," technology for the whole company, is threatened by ready technology since it can come and go so quickly, easily, and cost-effectively.

Ready technology also challenges our technology cost models, how we define and measure service level agreements (SLAs) and ultimately how we calculate technology TCO and ROI. Cost models, for example, based on buying, deploying, and supporting technology over a period of years are no longer relevant, as the definition of "ownership" morphs into "rent-instead-of-buy" deployment decisions. Devices such as tablets and smartphones are now treated as throwaways and nonrepairable assets. TCO models must adjust out the cost of buying and repairing technology; ROI models are more easily satisfied when unburdened by the acquisition of depreciable technology assets (as the overall cost of technology falls). SLAs must also be recalculated since technology delivery and support in most cases is provided completely by ready technology vendors.

Although there are still plenty of technologies that require traditional adoption processes, like big data analytics, enterprise resource planning (ERP) and customer relationship management (CRM) applications, there is a growing number of technologies ready to go to work immediately. Many of these technologies are cloud based, open source, and live happily outside of corporate firewalls. Many of them are easily and inexpensively accessible to corporate professionals and will therefore continue to find their way into companies of all shapes and sizes, regardless of what CIOs think about their readiness.

At the end of the day, ready technologies are upsetting just about every governance applecart at work today, as they rapidly discover, define, and solve more corporate problems. Rather than scramble to get all of the apples back in the cart, CIOs and chief technology officers (CTOs) should rethink the way useful technology enters the enterprise and embraces the role that ready technologies can play in the problem-solving process, especially since they have no choice.

References

"54% of Companies Ban Facebook, Twitter at Work," *Computerworld*, October 6, 2009.

Andriole, Stephen J. "7 Indisputable Trends That Will Define 2015," *Communications of the AIS*, January 2012a.

———. "Managing Technology in a 2.0 World," *IEEE ITProfessional*, January/February 2012b.

———. *The Transformation of Technology at Shire Pharmaceuticals*, Acentio Group, December 2012c.

———. *IT's All About the People Technology Management That Overcomes Disaffected People, Stupid Processes and Deranged Corporate Cultures*, Taylor & Francis, 2011.

———. "Business Technology Strategy in the Early 21st Century: Optimization through Rationalization," *Journal of Information Technology Research*, December 2010.

———. *Best Practices in Business Technology Management*, Auerbach, 2009a.

———. "Cloud Computing," *Cutter IT Journal: The Journal of Information Technology Management*, July 2009b.

———. *Technology Due Diligence: Best Practices for CIOs, Vendors and Venture Capitalists*, IGI, 2009c.

———. "The 7 Habits of Highly Effective Technology Leaders," *Communications of the ACM*, March 2007.

———. *The 2nd Digital Revolution: Candid Conversations About Business Technology Convergence*, IGI, 2005.

———. *Managing Systems Requirements: Methods, Tools and Cases*, McGraw-Hill, 1996.

———. *Rapid Applications Prototyping: The Storyboard Approach to User Requirements Analysis*, QED Information Sciences, 1992.

————. *Storyboard Prototyping: A New Approach to User Requirements Analysis*, QED Information Sciences, 1989.

————. (Ed.) "TACPLAN: An Intelligent Aid for Tactical Planning" in *Artificial Intelligence and National Defense: Applications to C31 and Beyond*, AFCEA International Press, 1987.

Athalye, Neeraj. "How Emerging Technologies Are Transforming the Retail Industry Vertical," *InformationWeek*, December 6, 2013 (http://www.informationweek.in/informationweek/perspective/286591/emerging-technologies-transforming-retail-industry-vertical).

Babcock, Charles. "Kaiser API Opens Healthcare Data to Mobile Apps," *InformationWeek*, June 3, 2013 (http://www.informationweek.com/mobile/kaiser-api-opens-healthcare-data-to-mobile-apps/d/d-id/1110219).

Benedict, Neal. "2014 Health IT Trends: Technology Set to Tackle Inefficiency in Healthcare," *Electronic Health Reporter*, December 2, 2013 (see http://electronichealthreporter.com/2014-health-it-trends-technology-set-to-tackle-inefficiency-in-healthcare/).

Bhasin, Kim. "Companies Around the World Are Banning Social Media Sites at Work More Than Ever," *Business Insider*, September 6, 2011 (http://articles.businessinsider.com/2011-09-06/strategy/30128243_1_social-media-social-sites-software-security-firm#ixzz2R42rosQA).

Braunstein, Mark. "Free the Data: APIs Boost Health Information Exchange," *InformationWeek*, January 27, 2014 (http://www.informationweek.com/%20healthcare/electronic-health-records/free-the-data-apis-boost-health-%20information-exchanged/d/d-id/1113579).

Brewin, Bob. "U.S. Lags the World's Top Adopters of Electronic Health Records Systems," *Nextgov*, September 22, 2009.

Bughin, Jacques, and Chui, Michael. "How Social Technologies Are Extending the Organization," *McKinsey Quarterly*, April 2011 (http://www.mckinsey quarterly.com/Business_Technology/How_social_technologies_are_extending_the_organization_2888).

Carr, Nicholas. *Does IT Matter?* Harvard Business School Press, 2004.

————. "IT Doesn't Matter," *Harvard Business Review*, May 1, 2003.

Currier, Guy. "Emerging Technology Adoption Trends in 2011," *CIO Insight*, January 3, 2011. (See more at: http://cioinsight.com/c/a/Research/Emerging-Technology-Adoption-Trends-for-2011-184380/#sthash.jKOnvacL.dpuf.)

Davidson, Kavitha A. "The Most Efficient Health Card Systems in the World (INFOGRAPHICS)," *The Huffington Post*, August 30, 2013.

Foley, John. "10 Technology Trends That Will Revolutionize Retail," *Forbes Magazine*, January 13, 2014 (http://www.forbes.com/sites/oracle/2014/01/13/10-technology-trends-that-will-revolutionize-retail/).

Gewirtz, David. "Top 5 Healthcare IT Trends to Look Out for in 2013," *ZDNet Health*, December 27, 2012 (http://www.zdnet.com/top-5-healthcare-it-trends-to-look-out-for-in-2013-7000009206/).

Horrigan, John. "Use of Cloud Computing Applications and Services," *Pew Internet and American Life Project*, September 12, 2008.

Joyce, William, Nohria, Nitin, and Roberson, Bruce. *What (Really) Works: The 4+2 Formula for Sustained Business Success*, Harper Business, 2003.

Kaneshige, Tom. "iPads in the Enterprise: IT Must Stay Ahead of the Curve," *CIO Magazine*, May 1, 2012 (http://www.cio.com/article/705379/).

Kroski, Ellyssa. "7 Ed Tech Trends to Watch in 2014," December 23, 2013 (http://oedb.org/ilibrarian/7-ed-tech-trends-watch-2014/).

Ludwig, Sean. "The iPad Is an Incredible Tool for Work—If Your IT Department Will Allow It," *VentureBeat*, January 4, 2012 (http://venturebeat.com/2012/01/04/ipad-enterprise-it/#sZBVhhB7uxj1vk4U.99).

Marchand, Donald A., and Peppard, Joe. "Why IT Fumbles Analytics," *Harvard Business Review*, January–February 2013.

Mithas, Sunil, Tafti, Ali, Bardhan, Indranil, and Goh, Jie Mein. "The Impact of IT Investments on Profits," *Sloan Management Review*, Spring 2012.

Moore, Geoffrey A. *Crossing the Chasm: Marketing and Selling High Tech Products to Mainstream Customers*, HarperCollins, 1991.

Murugesan, San. "Cloud Computing: A New Paradigm in IT," *Cutter Business Intelligence Executive Report*, Vol. 9, No. 2, 2009.

Nakamura, Gary. "Why Hadoop Only Solves a Third of the Growing Pains for Big Data," *Wired Magazine*, January 24, 2014 (http://www.wired.com/insights/2014/01/hadoop-solves-third-growing-pains-big-data/).

New Media Consortium (NMC) Horizon Report: 2014 Higher Education Preview, December 2013 (http://www.nmc.org/publications/2013-horizon-reporthigher-ed).

Orr, Ken, and Maher, Andy. "Here Comes Cloud Computing," *Cutter Consortium Business Technology Trends and Impacts Council Opinion*, Vol. 10, No. 1, 2009.

Ratchinsky, Karin. "Top HIT Trends for 2014: Accelerated Change Is Coming," *Healthcare IT News*, January 16, 2014 (http://www.healthcare-itnews.com/blog/top-hit-trends-2014-accelerated-change-coming).

Rogers, Everett M. *Diffusion of Innovations*, Free Press, 1962.

Rosoff, Matt. "Huge Construction Firm Uses iPads and Apple TV to Save Millions," *CITEWORLD*, March 28, 2013.

Savenije, Davide. "12 Tech Trends Higher Education Cannot Afford to Ignore," *Education Dive*, July 31, 2013 (http://www.educationdive.com/news/12-tech-trends-higher-education-cannot-afford-to-ignore/156188/).

"Top POS Predictions for 2014," *Retail Info Systems News*, December 17, 2013 (http://risnews.edgl.com/retail-trends/Top-POS-Predictions-for-201490104).

Vaquero, Luis M., Rodero-Merino, Luis, Caceres, Juan, and Linder, Maik. "A Break in the Clouds: Towards a Cloud Definition," *ACM SIGCOMM Computer Communication Review*, Vol. 39, No. 1, January 2009.

Worthen, Ben. "Start-Ups Emerge as Tech Vendors of Choice," *Wall Street Journal*, August 28, 2012.

Index

Printed and bound by CPI Group (UK) Ltd, Croydon, CR0 4YY

22/10/2024

01777622-0019